Good luck on 16th July
Love from Hugh

Fractured Society …
Causes, Effects and Resolutions
By
Hugh Roberts
ISBN: 978-1-8382223-2-1

GW00646222

Published By: -

i2i

PUBLISHING

i2i Publishing. Manchester.

www.i2ipublishing.co.uk

Author

Hugh Roberts has spent over forty years in planning, design and development consultancy for new towns and urban, industrial and regional infrastructure. He has lived, as well as worked, in all six continents with clients and project colleagues from many nationalities, characters and humours. He is a graduate of the Universities of Oxford and Wales.

Fractured Society ... Causes, Effects and Resolutions is his third book with the common denominator between each being an international perspective. *An Urban Profile of the Middle East*, published in 1979 and updated in 2016, did what it said on the cover. *Journeys with Open Eyes: Seeking Empathy with Strangers*, by i2i Publishing in 2017, was a travel biography, including interesting anecdotes about the people involved in urban master-planning for new towns and their infrastructure worldwide.

Hugh continues to do advisory work with a range of his former, full-time professional colleagues and lives in London with his wife Sylvie. They have two adult children, Mark and Shân and two granddaughters to date, Lola and Manon.

He is currently a Director of the Society of Authors and continues to travel widely for pleasure as well as urban project assignments.

Dedication

This book could be dedicated to so many people or experiences in my diverse life. I think though, I should go right back to my beginnings and dedicate it first to my parents, in recognition for having me, as I was taught to say leaving birthday parties when very small.

Mainly, I recognise their role in encouraging me, *'To get over the garden wall'* to reach out and explore the world in all its variety. Curiosity was the prime ingredient, to be interested in just about everything new, and hopefully therefore, having something interesting to say about it.

Thanks, Moyra and Reg, sadly no longer with us.

Then I should jump a couple of generations and make a further dedication to my grandchildren, who will be dealing bravely with the new world and its diverse societies that I describe here, long after I have gone.

With love to Lola and Manon, part of a generation with no idea of the pre-digital age, but still with lots of scope, *''To get over the garden wall'*.

Acknowledgements

These credits – static in books, rolling at the end of the average film - are too often the opportunity to list a vast range of people with whom to convey a subtle message of huge diligence as sources of reference. Academic books are often the worst perpetrators of this virtue signalling name-drop. While this book is not an academic treatise, I grapple with some complex life issues and I do so with whatever wisdom I have been able to glean as much through street wisdom as well as from books.

That does not stop me from listing a few strong influencers of what I believe in and what I have written about. Within the book and now here too, I pay tribute to my wife, Sylvie, who gives me a quiet but assured sense of context to so much in our lives. This is based extensively on the influence of her own father, Henri, with whom I had a strong understanding despite, or even because of, our different national and career backgrounds, as well as early life experience.

Teachers are always a strong influence on school kids and I could list many. But I will focus on just one - Ken Whitty - who taught me the basics of literary analysis for O Level English Language in 1966. He wrote a brilliant school play in 1968 on the thirtieth anniversary of the Munich Agreement between Chamberlain, Daladier and Hitler, titled *Appeasement is Fine, Peace in Our Time*. Tragically, he was killed in Athens in 1984, a victim of mis-identity by Palestinian terrorists.

Many of my bosses at work through five decades were inspirational. Peter Middleton kept everything together when Eurotunnel and TML were coming to blows over the Channel Tunnel project between 1986 and 1994. He was a personal mentor from whom I learned a lot, and a corporate diplomat in the first league, deserving of much more public recognition than he received.

My publisher, Lionel Ross, saw potential in my writing with my second book *Journeys with Open Eyes: Seeking Empathy with Strangers*, encouraging me to tackle a similar theme but in greater depth here.

Lionel's senior editor, Mark Cripps has kept me focused on the main purpose of each chapter towards a coherent single argument when I might have strayed. His patience and perseverance, as well as his chats about sport and the role it plays in socialising many people's lives, helped me when the spirit and motivation to complete this book were flagging.

Contents

Prologue

Fracture Alert

Human relationships have become fractured both physically and psychologically. But there is hope that they might be repaired if we adopt suitable responses as a society based on empathy and understanding.

*

I have a spent a lifetime living, working and latterly, just visiting many parts of the world where the greatest satisfaction has come from connecting with people. I don't just mean meeting and exchanging business cards or email addresses but making real connections with them that have turned into friendships. I cannot say these have all been lifelong relationships because we all move on. You can be friends forever, but also for a year, a week or just through fleeting acquaintance. But over whatever period, there seems, or seemed for a while, to be real understanding between us, despite a range of apparent cultural barriers – of language, politics, religion, gender, agenda and many more.

If asked to define the difference between mere acquaintance and real connections with people, my answer would be empathy. Now a much-overused word, empathy for me, amounts to imaginative identification with others, evidenced by starting to know things about someone without their having to spell them out. Of course, you can read the signals wrongly but that only increases the fascination of getting it right next time. Why? Because a world where we understand each other a little better is a better world, less prone to wrong conclusions, prejudices, hostility and ultimately, war. Not much to disagree with there, I hope.

It started with what my Mum said to me when young. Like her father before her, she believed strongly in people seeing the world, a belief encapsulated in urging me, "to get over the garden wall." And she did not mean visiting places just to put pins in a world map when back home, but to know people better from different cultures and therefore, viewpoints. That has been my mission since - to reach out beyond the comfort zone of the familiar and understand something of what and whom I find there. If there is any single rationale for this book, it is just that – triggering relationships with people to understand them better.

A pre-disposition to want to meet people, hear their story, or part of it at least, share some of mine and to be genuinely interested in variety of experience, has been essential. But my formula has always allowed for making mistakes. You learn as much from failure as success.

My chosen career reflected my quest. As an urban planner, I have worked across all six, permanently inhabited, continents, master planning new communities, industrial complexes and major urban infrastructure such as transport networks and water supplies. This takes a lot of explaining and mutual understanding to get it right, even with those who asked you to do it, because there are always more ways than one. Successful planning assesses the physical impacts of what will be built, how, where and when. Yet it starts and ends with understanding human aspirations.

There are an awful lot of stakeholders in any urban plan, starting and indeed finishing, with the people who will ultimately live there, but also various levels of government and private investors – all in it for their own definition of a return. The eventual inhabitants are the long-term stakeholders and they just seek a harmonious place to live. This imposes pressure to listen, learn and find an optimum path through conflicting interests. Getting over the garden wall indeed.

You gain a lot from listening and learning, and friendships are built along the way even with those whose objectives differ from your own. Successful projects are also dependent on forming effective teams and the ability to lead them well. So how you achieve your goals is as important as what they are because people remember you for how you respect their different objectives, thus determining successful outputs but the long-term outcomes as well. Or not. Remember, you learn as much from failure as success.

I counted everything from childhood upbringing through non work-related travels as essential training to acquire some skills in how to relate to people successfully. Most of us tend to separate travel for work with travel for pleasure, but even before I had chosen my future career, I was traveling and learning about groups, teams and leadership with which to find ways of doing things right when at last, the time came to plan new towns. Reaching beyond the garden wall? I would not have wanted to do anything else.

Acquisition of necessary life skills with which to make good judgements about people, their priorities and aspirations, is probably essential for almost any professional or technical endeavour. Hopefully, my experience is relevant to any career choice; its diversity certainly covers a wide range of circumstances, so there should be lots of common ground between yours and mine.

Just as I was completing my first draft of this book, the world was hit by the Coronavirus (CV19). There are no real modern precedents for CV19. Other pandemics such as SARS, MERS and Ebola spread within specific parts of the world before being more or less controlled, while CV19 is truly global and has yet to be controlled properly anywhere. Biologists who know about this stuff say that viruses never really go away; they might mutate or diminish below the level of our daily concern, but they are always there.

Over this last year, through 2020, our social contracts with each other have undergone huge changes and these will continue evolving, while the full impacts of CV19 are assessed. This is also true at the highest national and international level because such understanding ultimately depends on the success or failure of one-to-one relations between our leaders. Perhaps we can set them an example of how meaningful connections can be made from the individual level upwards, to promote a more harmonious world.

We have already voluntarily given up a wide range of civil liberties in an overwhelming acceptance of the need for collective action to fight this virus. Flexibility to changing conditions is what has brought our species through many past crises and will do so again. Social distancing has been the main ingredient of these changes, but my book reflects on the fact that through the use of social media, we had already started physically distancing from each other anyway.

We now have a vastly greater range of access to people worldwide, and this has provided limitless opportunity to understand the world better. But it is also false to assume that this amounts to more genuine relationships triggered between us. For one thing, there is a limit to the numbers of people with whom we can have meaningful connections at any one time. Secondly, I do not believe that most relationships commenced and filtered through an electronic device really amount to enduring friendship based on empathy and understanding. I elaborate on this in my first chapter, where I argue that we have been losing meaningful connection with people for the two or three decades since technology has given us the scope for alternatives to knowing people face-to-face. Whether by choice or more recent obligation, society may be drifting apart unless we can re-establish how to generate real understanding between us.

Looking back over the last year, it would have seemed scarcely imaginable to have written the previous paragraphs related to the impact of CV19 and pandemics in general. But that reminds me of two things. First, life is unpredictable, and its patterns impermanent, however familiar they may seem at the time. Secondly, my original purpose in writing the book does not need to be deflected, because the observations and conclusions I was already forming about fractured society may now be truer than ever. We have been drifting apart psychologically as well as physically, but CV19 also represents a big opportunity to press re-set on society's values as a longer-term response not only to pandemic but also building a kinder world.

I am not sure that online technology and digital communications make it so easy for generations now growing up to relate easily and well with people. This is because so many of their human interactions are indirect through a digital screen. I deal with this aspect of current education and experience in my first chapter. Real connections between people can never be achieved remotely, so re-learning how to relate to strangers face-to-face, is an essential skill for future generations. All generations seem to suffer to some extent and this chapter seeks to identify some of the main causes. The rest of my book picks the fractured society apart, examining individual ingredients of the problem, before my final chapters seek some formulae for a happier world.

After setting out my views on why young people seem more stressed than previous generations because of their sense of disconnectedness, I examine some of the ingredients for this fracture across society. The polarisation of political opinions such that we seem less able to agree to disagree, gender conflict between men and women, the changing dynamics of office environments, coping with trauma, and love or hate of places, all get an airing through my take on what has been happening these last five decades or more.

Maybe nothing really counts in connecting with people more than the unique contexts of when and how we meet up and relate to each other. That individuality of circumstance was important to record in my seventh chapter titled, 'Judgement in Context'. Every situation or encounter is unique and there are few guide rules. It was a tough chapter to write and relate to the rest, but critically important.

To provide some context for how I developed my own ways of connecting with people, my eighth chapter offers some biography about growing up and learning to get along with people - well most of them anyway - while avoiding the few psychopaths along the way. Psychos will always challenge the most benign of dispositions, but whether mild or profound, the symptoms they display are always there. You just have to find ways of living with them.

My penultimate chapter is something of an encounter guide, offering ideas for meeting new people, places and cultures for the first time. As a kind of to-do list, there are just as many what not to-do's there, based on my many errors along the way. I called it, 'Meeting people halfway'. We will lose that facility at our peril.

Not quite finally, I then offer my views on how we can build a better world titled, 'Getting along with nearly everybody'. I conclude that there is scope in our hyper-communicated world for making a better job of connecting with each other in social as well as medical pandemic conditions. That once meant how to deal with everyone when those meetings were all held face-to-face. But now that is also possible and commonplace digitally. We need to keep in focus the big picture about what humanity is all about, a section I call, 'Love, Life and the Pursuit of Happiness'.

I finish with an Epilogue which is an end piece recommending some simple but challenging things that we can do to make the world a better place after CV19.

Having encountered and worked with so many diverse people and situations and survived with a smile to tell the tale, I remain optimistic that human nature is the most powerful force for good. I hope you will read on, motivated by that optimism. My recipe for life relationships offers a range of happy endings to be found if you know where, how and what to look for.

The purpose of this book is to examine why this is needed and how perhaps we might just find it.

Chapter 1

Youth under Stress

Young people today are stressed and living in an environment where digital media and devices have become the norm when they are connecting and communicating with each other. This situation is not building meaningful relationships.

*

Our world is awash with angst and uncertainty about life's purpose. Millennials and particularly that younger generation who came of age in the first two decades of the twenty-first century, seem afflicted with a higher level of depression than hitherto.

We are all stressed, but young people in particular, living in a social environment dominated by digital media and handheld communication devices. The instant gratification of acquiring things combined with not relating to friends and family as we used to face-to-face, is generating a fractured and discontented society. CV19 has increased the sense of dislocation, but its impacts may point the way to solutions for the future.

Historical perspective on stress

Of course, older generations were not immune to stress, and with good reason. Until only seventy years ago, so within many people's living memory, life expectancy, even in developed economies, was just about that - seventy years, or three score years and ten as the Bible puts it. Full cures for some of the most debilitating diseases were rare, so even if you did not die of them, your quality of life might be severely degraded. Seventy years ago, people were still remembering vividly the most lethal and widespread World War and undergoing the painful re-building process of both social and built infrastructure after the mass destruction suffered not only by the defeated but by most of the victors too. And a new threat of nuclear war was emerging with at least the technical possibility of total annihilation. Judging by the levels of mistrust that had grown rapidly between former allies against fascism and Nazism, Armageddon never seemed far away. Cold War was replacing the hot variety, but the menace remained.

Yet those of us who grew up through the two subsequent decades were a pretty optimistic lot who managed to separate the world's problems and threats from our personal lives and loves. I recall the twin superpower stand-offs between the US and its allies and the Soviet Union as close encounters with nuclear annihilation, but with a sense of detachment. For example, the events of October 1962 in Cuba, or November 1983 in Germany for NATO's misunderstood Able Archer military exercises and the Warsaw Pact's paranoid response through Operation Ryan, seemed beyond our control or were over before we fully realized their menace. I took cold comfort from my dad's philosophy from World War II; if the bullet had your name on it, then there was little you could do, so quit worrying. Of course, the Armageddon bullet would have been for all of us, but that only seemed to depress a small minority. Despite evidence to the contrary, most of us sang and danced through the 1960s, perhaps as if those days were our last. They say if you remembered them you were not there - another way of coping, probably.

Life expectancy through these decades was improving steadily as better nutrition, effective medical science and more important, the widespread application of both, impacted our lifestyles. We were progressively stubbing out the cigarettes, monitoring heart disease for prevention rather than cure and letting medical research make big inroads into combating cancers, still one of the biggest threats to health, but nothing compared to a previous generation. And these advances were not the exclusive preserve of the modern economies of the First and Second World, as we then defined them. The so-called Third or developing World was benefitting too, from lower infant mortality, mass inoculation, better nutrition and if not more stable peace-time governments, then at least, a growing sense of self, rather than colonial-style social evolution.

These are not just rosy impressions from my own youth in denial of the geopolitical menace. Professor Hans Rosling in his excellently researched 2018 book *Factfulness: Ten Reasons we're wrong about the world - And why things are better than you think*, charts a wide range of key measures of the way in which the world is so much better off than seven decades ago. If you need some cheerful truths, go read it.

So, what has changed to render us all, but millennials and younger folk, more vulnerable to depression, suicide and the range of mental insecurities that lead up to them? Are they part of a snowflake generation that worries excessively about everything, or is it something more profound? We who grew up in the 1960s, were also branded soft by our parents' generation who had faced the rigours of war, so I suspect the snowflake label is as unfair now as we considered ours to be then.

A decline in relative happiness
Measuring happiness and wellbeing is far from simple. In fact, populations taken as a whole, seemed until very recently, to have been getting happier in the last two to three decades, probably reflecting those improvements in health, nutrition and economic opportunities worldwide. That is, until CV19, knocked all our perceptions of happiness or stress for six. But it is far too soon to be trying to measure change from something

only months old, however profound has been its impact. It is still just possible that a gradual improvement in the extent of infection and associated death rates, followed by a similar resurgence of the economy, might mean that CV19 has a relatively short-term impact on society. I doubt it, somehow, but on this question, we must wait.

From the pre-CV19 world, take the work of Esteban Ortiz-Ospina and Max Roser at Oxford University's Martin School who, in their *Happiness and Life Satisfaction* report of 2017 measured the proportions of people in ninety-nine countries worldwide who felt 'rather' or 'very' happy. They deliberately adopted a simple five-point scale from not happy to very happy, thus smoothing out cultural differences between diverse national samples. They found significant upward trends in the happiest two categories, most of them from high seventy per cents to the low eighty per cents. Given such a large statistical framework these are significant increases and it is the scale of the shift upwards rather than the absolute numbers that are important. Some countries achieved spectacular increases such as Russia up from only forty-seven per cent in 1995 to nearly seventy-four per cent in 2014 – probably related to apparently better economic or political conditions during that time, while others, like Sweden have only been flat-lining because their scores in the mid ninety per cents could hardly go higher. So, despite the need to qualify such data heavily for so-called optimism or language biases etc, this is surely one of many proofs positive, that general material improvements in people's lives have been broadly correlated with greater happiness.

Yet, in stark contrast to trends in the overall population, young people seem to be experiencing an increased level of unhappiness. Take the *World Happiness Report* published by the Sustainable Development Solutions Network sponsored by six major private sector companies and philanthropists and published by three prestigious academic institutions in the UK and North America. They quote a US survey of General Happiness of eighth, tenth and twelfth graders (from thirteen to eighteen years old) reflecting a marked fall off of life satisfaction starting from 2006 and continuing for eleven years to 2017 when the most recent measures were taken. If the US is not sufficiently representative of the youth of the world, take the UK's Children's Society reflected in their *Good Childhood Report* of 2019, which recorded a four per cent decline in their Mean Happiness Ratio from 2009 to 2017. That may not seem a huge change but given the typically large size of sampling of these measures and the opposite trends in the population, they are significant.

What is important here is the fact that these age groups also represent the cohorts of our population that are already now the young adults of today, soon to become the opinion formers of tomorrow as their careers, lifestyles and expenditures come to dominate economic and social trends. To have identified stress patterns for young people that are counter-indicative to overall population happiness, is indeed worrying. Will they also come to reflect morale for all our futures?

Given that I base my arguments on a pre CV19 world, I believe there have been two big long-term culprits for the heightened state of stress that we, but young people in particular, are experiencing; one that applies society-wide and the other equally ubiquitous but felt at a deeply personal level.

The drive to acquire more stuff
The first modern but deep-rooted source of stress is the endless demands of materialism, the lust to acquire things. This is stressful in itself because of the constant fear of missing out – so called FOMO. But since 2009, with reduced personal credit available from banks, the combination of wanting but not

getting, has become acute for a large proportion of the population. The second source of stress has been the explosion in easily available hand-held digital communication devices. Now add to these, the long-term changes wrought by our currently dystopian CV19 circumstances, in particular, close contact with others - or what we might call - fear of going out – or FOGO. And it is safe to say that the malign effects of materialism and disconnectedness are not going to improve any time soon.

The excessive materialism creating our heightened sense of insecurity sets up a toxic chain reaction. It starts with our need to acquire things and ends when we realize that the satisfaction from doing so is merely temporary. Unhappiness by any other definition, this amounts to a feeling among too many people of being left behind by the material advances of others. And it is contagious, with the anxiety spreading from the most materialistic to those who would not regard themselves as needing lots of possessions, but who react to the unhappiness in those that do by thinking 'why not me too?'

A philosophical or even religious perspective might be useful here. Christians are not great on the happiness thing, although some evangelicals seem to embrace it. Love gets top billing - good news for any searcher after how to connect with people - but the happiness thing seems to have been better dealt with by the Buddhists. You will have to look elsewhere for in-depth analysis of Buddhist philosophy, but bear with me on this for a paragraph or two while I try to explain.

According to Buddha, there are four Noble Truths leading the way via a further Eightfold Path to peace of mind (nirvana) as the real source of happiness. The first three Truths deal with dysfunctions as the mental root of unhappiness, based primarily on cravings of the senses for material possessions, and how to eliminate these. The fourth Truth maps out a subsequent

Eightfold Path to happiness through wisdom to know oneself, behave ethically and to cultivate the mind to a state of grace to overcome the cravings. I confess to a lack of mental discipline to resist some of those cravings and thus remain lost in the foothills of the uphill route to nirvana. A wretched creature like most of humanity, I might, nonetheless, know enough to appreciate my thoroughly non-transcendent state. That puts me a little further down the self-awareness road than some perhaps, but not by much. But one thing should be evident from all this. Unhappiness is engendered by the continuous pursuit of worldly goods and continuous gratification of the senses. Let's build on that widely accepted fact.

The enlightenment referred to by Buddhist theology might be summed up in a few words as being content within one's own skin – the contentment to know that the world is a beautiful place, all of its creatures whether human or not having a place in it and a destiny to fulfil. Thinking about our unique place in the world and changing behaviour to match are two different things of course, but the idea is a start. There are too few of us who can fully attain this state of non-materialist grace, but its absence creates different vacuums in people. In the worst cases, it amounts to an echoing void – what the main religions might describe as a loss of soul.

As an alternative to nirvana, the ownership of stuff gives a temporary sense of self-worth. It was bread and circuses for the citizens of Ancient Rome, now it might be a new car every couple of years, a new wide screen TV or another holiday just weeks after the last.

The drying up of credit - until recently
Before 2008, and the Global Financial Crisis (GFC), credit was easily obtained – probably too easily. If your neighbour paid cash for his new car, you could easily do the same on credit. Who

cared how it was paid for? Credit? A mere detail! But you felt good about 'keeping up with the Jones's'. You could get the feel-good factor easily and let the future liability look after itself later.

With stricter bank lending after the worldwide GFC bailouts of 2009-10, such consumer indulgence became a lot more difficult - good for long term family budgeting perhaps, but effectively denying the immediate pleasure rush. Perhaps as well, the dearth of credit might have forced the next-door Jones's to reflect whether a new car was necessary, or might it be wiser to make do with their ten-year-old Daihatsu.

In Victorian times and probably through the first half of the twentieth century, poor people had limited expectations of the good things of life. They were simply out of reach. But what you did not have you largely did not miss. In the free spending late 1980s, 1990s and noughties meanwhile, consumer goods and buying each new dose of good sensations was visible to all via the broadcast media, becoming the norm for far too many of us. A lot of the buying was on credit, but once the access to worldly goods had been tasted, it was doubly hard to lose. This loss that I might term consumerism denied, was felt deeply.

A sense of entitlement soon converts to a sense of self-righteous injustice. The impression lurks in the sub-conscience that others are still enjoying the benefits of those worldly goods - wall-to-wall advertising sees to that. The loss of easy credit rendered the gratification of consumerism unobtainable to those without access to the cash or credit.

If consumer credit was tougher to find, the same was, until recently, the case for corporate finance. Companies could not borrow easily, except with more stringent asset cover. So, although current profit and loss account business recovered in many western economies after 2010 (explaining why we had relatively full employment), until the last few months and the onset of CV19, the sense of risk taking with longer term investments via wider borrowing had been significantly curtailed.

Since 2008, until very recently, governments felt they should lead by example and not borrow like they used to. Towards the end of an electoral cycle where future votes could be weighed alongside future public expenditure commitments, parties in power would typically spend on improving public services. But since the GFC, austerity has been the main response – again, until very recently. With more stringent credit restrictions, and the need to set an example, governments in many countries, adopted low spend policies across public sector services, especially and perhaps fatally now for so many who have died of CV19, within health services.

Governments reined in expenditure on public health and education or building new hospitals or schools, together with tighter funding conditions for new built infrastructure such as transport links. Meanwhile care for the elderly and vulnerable deteriorated, and grants or loans to kick start economic investment in new industries and urban infrastructure dried up. One of the biggest stress impacts imposed by spending cuts between 2010 and 2020 were reductions in policing, giving a boost to drug-based organised and increasingly violent crime. This was able to flourish with relative impunity from detection and sanction because of cuts in policing.

Now so much of this has been changed. Since the devastating impact of CV19, we are faced with the first collapse of economic activity in living memory for reasons other than financial confidence. No one fully understands this and how it will play out. The collapse has been profound as we fight contagion, exceeding in magnitude and abruptness, the decline in economies after the Great Depression from late 1929 and through much of the subsequent 1930s.

Paradoxically, my previous arguments about credit being so hard to access have now been turned on their head. Governments have been forced to make access to credit hugely easier just to keep economic wheels turning discernibly. This is unlikely to do anything to make access to personal credit and wider economic growth any easier. For the first time in global history, economies have fallen off a cliff edge as large parts of working life have stopped to keep people a safe distance from each other. Almost all other economic crises have been financially driven by a loss of confidence that markets would continue to grow. Confidence in the economy had less to do with the immediate post CV19 shutdowns than combating contagion, but it will be critical to whether we will make a long-term recovery swiftly, more slowly - or at all. No one knows for sure and those who make confident predictions should be viewed with scepticism.

So, the last ten years have been far from easy for many people, particularly for those coming of age during that decade. And now, one other thing is certain: CV19 makes no one happier.

Human connections through a filter

My next culprit for the long-term senses of stress in younger people is a more personal one. It is derived from the availability of cheap hand-held digital communication devices. Put simply, young people don't talk to each other enough anymore, other than through the distorting filter of their mobile phones or other easily obtainable IT devices.

We used to consider such mass communication with optimism. Nearly three decades ago, around about the publication of Francis Fukuyama's book *The End of History and the last Man* in 1992 while the communist regimes of central and eastern Europe were collapsing, we thought that mass communication in everyone's hands would destroy the ability of future autocratic governments to return to oppressive and anti-democratic behaviours. If injustices were being done, someone would find out about them and report to the world in a manner which society would discover at the touch of a button and governments could not suppress. Democracy would follow this onset of transparency and only those governments that played fair with their citizens would prevail.

To an extent, the principle of such whistleblowing has been realized, and not just governments, but large corporations and quasi-governmental organisations are now much more circumspect about how they conduct themselves. Transparency and democracy for all? Well not quite.

Listen only to the news you want to hear
Widespread digital communication has also led to manipulation of the news and the means of circulating it via access to the Internet. If you cannot suppress news that undermines your cause, invent smokescreens. Fake news probably started merely to defame but has evolved in a malign direction to become a device masking real news of the sort that one agency or another does not want us to know about. Generate lots of fake stuff that progressively no one believes, and you effectively camouflage much of the bad news that is true but can be branded fake because there's so much of both varieties around. Who will tell the difference?

Fake news is now common practice in the trading of information, to a greater extent than in previous generations when its predecessor - propaganda - was the curated task of whole governmental ministries. So now, at the same time as we are absorbing new information, we are also subconsciously asking, 'Who is telling me this?' And if it comes from a source we suspect as partisan for or against a particular cause, our response is a cynical, "Well, they would say that, wouldn't they?" always assuming we can identify the source in the first place.

For a lot of what we learn, the medium and its source have become more important than the message itself. This leads inexorably, to our accepting what we want to believe because of who is telling it to us and discounting the rest. News has become a matter of choice.

This is mirrored by trends in the entertainment industry. Broadcast entertainment used to be viewed on the few available TV channels by multiple millions, such that it was discussed widely the next day in the market place, the Post Office queue or during the office tea break, with high expectations that everyone had been watching. We shared impressions and cultural influences. Now, so called terrestrial TV is challenged and eclipsed by online services such as Netflix, Apple TV or Amazon Prime where you view precisely what you want when you want it (at a price). We all, but especially post-millennials, now consider this entirely natural. But my point is not that it is worse than when entertainment was served up in a take-it-or-leave-it form, but rather that there was previously little choice. It was a set menu, not à la carte.

So not only news, but diversions from it are now also a matter of choice – to be exposed to and absorbed or not. This seems seductively liberal in concept, giving choosers all the scope necessary to think for themselves, having researched or browsed different data, messages, or storylines. But choice is also bewildering, because we rarely know how wide it really is, so we tend to opt for the comfortable and familiar. You have to be very disciplined and almost obsessively objective to do otherwise. Intellectual laziness is wholly understandable in a communication-rich world. Why test your assumptions about the right answer or how things might be done differently when affirmation that you were right all along is so much more gratifying? Given that there is so much information out there, most of which I don't know about and therefore cannot trust, why should I question what I know from my own experience and gut feeling? In other words, I already know best!

I often think that to keep a lively mind, I should access the news source (hard copy or online) whose political views I broadly dis-agree with. Isn't open debate all about testing my views against those of others? Instead, we tend to cleave to one news medium on the grounds that we know our way around and are familiar with its columnists' ways of arguing their case. However, there is then a tendency to become mirror images not only of their thinking but the underlying values from which that thinking evolves. Five minutes of current affairs conversation with a fellow Brit and I think I can tell which newspaper they read. Comfort dominates but curiosity dies a little, every time surrounding views affirm our own.

So, far from opening us up to a wider world of diverse stimuli, choice promoted by online access has all too easily baffled us into retreat to what is familiar. I believe this is giving rise to real entrenchment of views and politics at a more visceral scale than for many decades previously. I elaborate on this in the next chapter.

Of course, there are huge advantages to be gained from easy online access in terms of the way we can reach out, stay in touch and sustain contacts with events and personal relationships with people globally. Just as important, the easy access afforded by online links to sorting the most mundane of procedural tasks has transformed our lives over recent decades. This applies not only to news updates, but to shopping, bank account monitoring and transactions, insurance or license renewal, weather forecasts, route guidance, rooting out general knowledge or casual dictionary references, all the way to conducting academic research and running whole businesses. Life on a screen, but at a price – information curated for us rather than fashioned for ourselves.

Blurring of the public and private realms

There are many more learned studies than mine about how broadcast media and digital communication has changed youthful perceptions of their world. Many of these are already well advanced in years, few more so than that of Jürgen Habermas who in 1969 wrote a seminal work on *Structural transformation of the public sphere: an inquiry into a category of Bourgeois society*. Even the best academic paper I found (and most readable - many are not) by social psychologist Sonia Livingstone of LSE, called *In defence of privacy: mediating the public/private boundary at home* is now fifteen years old. These works record the fact that even within the nuclear family, the divisions between the public and private realm were shifting with the mass media encroachments of the late twentieth century. By 2005, Livingstone could state that the digital media we all now take for granted were more readily accessed by children than their parents. Early adoption of IT skills compared with older generations was earning children the right to determine some of the conditions of their association with adults. "You don't know as much as me about how to access stuff online, so you are going to have to trust me!" they could claim.

The trends observed a decade and a half ago have only been reinforced with time. Driven by a natural desire to participate in social interaction with their friends, children accept and rely on digital media to play a dominant role in their lives. Identity development is fully bound up with and mediated by music, sport, fashion, and lifestyle consumerism, and the resulting enhancement of personal images often falls short of high expectations leading to stress, anorexia, cyber bullying and depression. Yet children's ready access to a digital public domain before entering its physical equivalent has meant that they become media savvy long before attaining the maturity to understand digital literacy needed to protect their own privacy and rights. And that is before we even consider their psychological well-being!

It is a bewildering paradox that children are simultaneously growing up faster through the impact of what they access online while staying younger for longer as they do so in isolation of others while in front of their screens. Little wonder there are such high levels of stress among teenagers growing up, to which adults need to respond with empathy and understanding.

Perfecting the personal image only for reality to fall short
Access to personal intercommunications is probably where the greatest youthful stress is being generated, eroding broadly positive views of the world and trust in our fellow man. What we feel privately, we quickly express publicly. Few of us are fully discreet. We now spend hours a day on our hand-held or otherwise portable devices, leaving little time for and even blocking out face to face interaction with everyone from mere acquaintance through to members of close family. So called connectedness is conducted too often at one remove via internet transmitted, word processed, and thus carefully modulated media. A lot of this is monologue not dialogue.

The worst of online messaging is that it stifles debate. After a few exchanges, people stop playing email or Twitter tag, when an equivalent face-to-face conversation might go on for hours. When you speak to someone face to face, you expect spontaneous response whether agreeing, disagreeing, or at least challenging you to justify what you have just said. If you are lucky, there will be lots of good-natured banter in between, making the whole experience an enjoyable one. With digital media meanwhile, observation of body language, facial expression and the way words are voiced rather than typed into comprehensible speech, are all wholly absent. You simply have no clues as to how your correspondent is really feeling or reacting to what you write. Given that our species used to experience most of what it learned via visual communication, together with smell, taste and touch rather than the spoken or written word, we are, in the space of one generation, undergoing major psychological changes to the way we react to others and thus interact with them.

The IT geeks who have served up these media are well aware of the absence of facial or body language messages and have come up with their solution - the emoji! These cosy images were originally just smiley faces for kids to play around with and to show good intent - that you were only joking. But as texting also invites brevity (no bad thing in itself), the emoji has taken over across all generations replacing expressions of ever more complex emotions – anger or rage, impatience, awe, love, jealousy, doubt, wry amusement and more. How did the emoji artists capture all or any of those in a tiny face image? But they did, and a raft of others as well - but on their own terms of course. Seems now that you don't even need words to message; there is an emoji somewhere to reflect your mood.

Consider what this is doing to our sense of connectivity to each other. On the plus side, we can communicate instantly with vastly more people anywhere in the world than was ever possible before - provided they are awake. And because we can use these technologies, we will – one of the immutable laws of 'progress'. Not only can we communicate but we send photographs, videos with musical accompaniment and professional standard editing, accompanied by lots of other carefully crafted media to update on our social life, career achievements, eating regimes, sporting prowess, latest social life - and worse.

Too much information, indeed. Not because it is bad to keep in touch with news and views, but mainly because it rapidly leads to sensory overload. Most of us cannot cope with the sheer weight of new information that we never asked for nor received before. And the loss is a loss of real relationships to be replaced by an ersatz variety processed for us through digital technology as well as a large dose of the sender's vanity.

Even benign messaging can become cloying. We rapidly make adverse judgements about those who insist on telling us of their latest holiday, achievements at work or play, and even their latest meal out, not to mention (and sometimes less benign) their latest loves or sexual conquests. Unconsciously, we know how carefully curated these messages have been to ensure best foot forward and that any indignities are only presented as self-deprecatory humour. The distant rumble that this is all fake news may be suppressed because we sense the person is not like that, but the medium of the message is the bit that often grates. And no one can hide unless they unsubscribe and to do that often feels like writing yourself out of the circle. Not a good social strategy.

The dark side of the messaging moon
Messaging becomes malign when the tone and motivation shifts from positive to negative. Mild criticism or laughing at someone else's funny habits is easily enough dealt with face-to-face. But online, we suddenly lose control of where messages are going and stress excessively that self-image is being tarnished. We are all entitled to a modicum of respect from others, the better to achieve self-respect as the precursor to self-confidence. So, this concern with personal image is not vanity, at least not to start

with. But precisely because we are not in control of the message and where it is going, we react differently to digital teasing than its face-to-face alternative.

As messaging turns negative, it can soon tip over into cyber-bullying, subtle and wheedling to start with but with scope to become something more threatening. Young people are particularly vulnerable to this electronic bear pit. And they are often understandably shy of calling it out when it starts. What used to be physical or merely mental, but still face-to-face, bullying has gone online. Playing on people's unaccountable fears is now all too easy by revealing other people's indiscretions that are not in themselves ruinous, but nonetheless erode self-confidence.

For example, pursuit of physical perfection has become an obsession with some young people not yet exposed to the evidence of ageing. With so many carefully crafted comparators to view with symmetrical faces, expertly coiffed hair, contact lens-enhanced eye colour, pouting lips, perfect legs, six pack stomachs, pert boobs, oil-drop, or silicone injected behinds depending on gender preference. No wonder we all fall short.

Sadly, personality or physical character trashing does not always stop at the level of minor indiscretions. The cyber bully only really gets into his or her stride when complete assassination of reputation becomes the purpose. Porn shaming and publishing intimate photos of (usually ex) partners online is just one example. The dark web where child pornography and the means to enable malicious stalking, reside are more damaging still. And the carefully selected witnesses to the malign message – via blind copy - do not even need to be present altogether, as for physical bullying. Bullies usually like an audience except for sinister one-to-one threats, so blind copying is a perfect device to ensure a victim's pain. Destruction of confidence as the message drip-drips slowly into people's consciences is the inevitable result. Little wonder, that this invisible force sometimes leads to suicidal thoughts and - tragically – suicidal realities.

For those who have not experienced cyber bullying, my account may sound like exaggeration, despite its being very real for far more young people than confess to it. But for those of us of older generations, consider one comparable behaviour pattern from the familiar world of driving a car. When we meet people in the street, we are usually polite so as to convey a good impression or at least not to cause offence. But wrapped around within the metal box of our cars, our behaviour becomes more aggressive. The difference? The sense of detachment from people. That is precisely why so much bullying has gone online; because it can, and the bully feels secure from sanction; as for the false bravery of road rage, so for the isolation of cyber bullying.

I focus on the malign effects of digital communication as my second major source of unhappiness in young people. My third may well come to eclipse the previous two, but I remain optimistic that it will not.

Unexpectedly better after Coronavirus?

Several months into CV19 impacts, we have taken those IT skills and technologies we have learned over the last two decades to a wholly new level, as we explore how to maintain our societies and economies without physical contact under virus spread lockdown. What used to require physical presence and associated long journeys, taking hours or days to be present in person to conduct individual business procedures, now takes minutes, releasing us from the drudgery of so much mundane bureaucracy. While this excludes and marginalizes a shrinking minority of those with no digital access, for the great majority of the population for whom the real cost of hand-held devices diminishes annually, the liberation from time-consuming tasks ought to be inspiring. So much more time available for more creative activity, not forgetting the de-stressing effects of doing nothing at all.

But pre CV19, this liberation had not yet induced a more relaxed mood, waves of fresh creativity or a wider sense of mental wellbeing. On the contrary, we filled our time with self-imposed demands to get more things done, expecting instant access, instant response and instant results en route, such that the tiniest delay generated acute frustration. Dealing with technological devices on a one-to-one basis, away from the knockabout world of human interaction has bred in us all a level of self-absorption and focused entitlement that renders us less sociable. Now that the use of online and digital communication has temporarily replaced the face-to-face kind so comprehensively during lockdowns, our dependency on it has become total. This is changing our mental map of humanity.

When online messaging first became ubiquitous, it seemed like a new 'deus ex machina' of unexpected power to liberate us from temporal and geographical limits, offering us the world as a potential audience and mouthpiece at touch of the device's multiple buttons. But instead, digital connection has become a kind of 'homines ex machina' in which we are placing false belief that filtering real communication through a handheld gizmo gives us the world and choice at our fingertips. In purely messaging terms, it does just that, but at the price each time of a little bit of our humanity.

Those experiencing the stress and uncertainty about where they stand in the world may just be the precursors of wider dissatisfaction with the loss of meaning from human relations, based on an absence of empathy with our fellow beings. When we add fake news to the communication-rich atmosphere, the scope for simple answers to single problems becomes seductive. In the absence of proper dialogue, our powers of judgement are progressively diminishing. Our mental health is at stake.

The abrupt sense of isolation induced by separating people to reduce virus infection may just have re-awakened in us the understanding that we need more from communication than merely the written word on the hand-held device. Since the onset of CV19, many have come to realise that we must first connect properly to be able to live together in harmony – to generate what I called in my Prologue, meaningful connections.

It is common to measure the cultural foundations of society by the outputs of our minds, bodies and creativity – philosophy, art, music, sport and, in my area of endeavour, great places to live. But there is a more fundamental foundation than any of these and that is togetherness – the ability to get along with each other. This stimulates the genius in us to create the physical or mental expressions of our culture which we otherwise take for granted. They are not the building blocks but the outputs and outcomes of culture. What sustains them is our ability to work together and catalyse the creativity in the first place. We lose this to the seductive appeal of remote working and distant communing with each other at our peril.

Human relations are the stimulus that has sustained our species for thousands of years, sometimes for ill, but primarily for good. Far too much of this stimulus has now been replaced by a flickering screen and an emoji as a poor substitute for a real smiling face or the kindness of touch and feel. In a current social environment of even more profound isolation, the shock to our mental health may now be more apparent than ever.

This opening chapter has been unrelentingly downbeat in terms of what I believe may be happening to society. But the last part of my introductory message will be positive, because in every crisis and problem, however profound, there is opportunity. It sometimes takes psychological shock to make us reconsider our real values, as Alvin Toffler reflected in his seminal work *Future Shock* in the mid-1980s. Toffler's main arguments concerned the growth of globalisation, while the recent isolation imposed by CV19 might be seen as a counterweight to global trends. But emerging from CV19 and navigating away from previously unprecedented levels of social isolation, we have time to reflect on two things.

The first is that the materialist pursuit of stuff is less important for any of us than good relations; stuff does not provide a lasting feelgood factor, but good relations do. Secondly, while the digital revolution is currently maintaining us in those relationships albeit at a distance, they can never be a permanent solution to the way we achieve lasting and meaningful connections between us. We need to reach out to friends, family and new acquaintances far more effectively than that. It may just now be possible that the recent universal shock of CV19 to our psychological well-being, will act as a catalyst to achieving a better world.

Excess materialism has generated a sense of gratification denied and digital communication is robbing us of direct human interaction to understand the elements of happiness at the face-to-face level. However, through the shock to our mental health of CV19, we have now received an unprecedented wake-up call to re-examine the value systems that have brought us to this place. If we do this examination carefully, it will make us better able to reject the worst and exploit the best qualities of what constitutes meaningful connections in society.

My next five chapters address different aspects of the fractured society. Five decades of living and working on urban development projects in diverse communities worldwide, master planning new towns, industrial complexes and urban infrastructure have provided my motivation for finding empathy with others. In my last few chapters, I explain how finding the ways to really connect with other people, where there are also major cultural differences to transcend, has been for me, one of the most satisfying journeys to be making through life. They are just my impressions alone but given the depth of relationship building to address such tasks, and the diversity of cultures with which I worked, I hope they will strike chords with others despite contrasting experience.

Chapter 2

Polarised Politics

Politics has become polarised around major issues in a way that is dividing people across families and friends at one end of the spectrum, all the way to the other end, where national and international relations are affected. Deepening disagreements, often amounting to hatred, are the product of a gulf of misunderstanding. For all its brilliant capacity to enable communications, the digital world and the internet bear much of the responsibility.

*

We define ourselves more readily by what we are not than what we are. Almost everyone knows a lot about what they don't like - poverty, illness, disease, family disharmony, to list merely the most obvious. But when it comes to saying what we do like and how to achieve it, then it gets a little harder to be specific beyond broad generalities.

An old Welsh joke from my home describes poor Dai who had been shipwrecked on a desert island for five years before being rescued by the Navy. As the ship's lighter pulls away from the beach, the naval lieutenant asks him why he had built a chapel on one headland and another on the other. "Oh well," Dai replies pointing them out in turn, "That is the one I go to and that is the one I don't go to!"

Knowing what we do not want out of life is easy enough, but understanding and thus being able to define what we do want is very difficult, as good careers teachers will explain, when they interview young people ready to leave school or college. Beyond the self-evident preferences to be healthy and financially comfortable, the things that people want from life seem almost too non-specific to be put into thought or word. The same goes for values of a less quantifiable nature. It is almost as if specifying one aspiration implies exclusion of others, or perhaps, the shyness not to be seen to want all of one's cake and eat it.

This chapter looks at our perception that political debate about what people want for themselves and expect from governments seems to have become so much more visceral in recent years. Likes and dislikes are no longer mildly expressed preferences but a part of identity. And identity is perceived as under threat, unless it is defined minutely not just for what it is but what it is not.

"This is where I stand. Are you with me or against me?" The absence of anything in between either with or against is the sea change since a more tolerant time when people might have been prepared to accept differences and rub along together. This is not new; there have been periods of intolerance in the past but current expressions of it seem to exist globally if not universally. Is there any way back from this and if so how?

Style or substance in leadership?
The challenge to making suitable life choices and then living by them alone, extends into our dislikes among political viewpoints and more so the people who represent them. We spend an inordinate time observing and criticising politician X or party Y's message and his or her means of delivering it. We probably all agree that leadership is essential in almost every human endeavour, but few of us seem to agree on what constitutes the ingredients of a good leader. A bit like beauty perhaps, we recognise it when we see it but struggle to define its key elements. Even such fundamentals for leadership as the capacity to make decisions and act upon them, surely essential in any implementable plan, are pored over and criticised for being too

measured or too swiftly entered into or arrived at and by means not wholly approved of.

Such criticism usually originates from those who disagree fundamentally with the measures adopted – for them neither medium nor message are right. But even those who agree fundamentally with a given course of action, will often question how it was achieved, suggesting a different route either out of personal vanity or because the medium or means of doing something is as important as the message or action itself. Politicians can rarely win for long, as we judge them for style as much as substance. Worse still for their valediction, their careers are largely defined by the pursuit of power, such that when it is lost, only a sense of failure remains. Politicians rarely appreciate as they climb the greasy pole to power that almost all their careers end in failure to the extent that they eventually bequeath that power. They really need some other motivation for their political careers to compensate for that loss.

These passing preferences or dislikes for those that rule us seemed once to be just that, passing observations about style from which we gradually moved on to the next issue. In most openly democratic countries, few died because this party or that was in power, bones were only broken in exceptional circumstances and anyway, there was much else to worry about and even enjoy in life beyond politics.

That is a huge privilege compared with more autocratic regimes, who seek to impose their will on every aspect of citizens' lives. We who enjoy democratic means to depose tyrannical rule need to be reminded that further back in our own national history our ancestors suffered mightily from the imposition and retention of power. This can happen again unless we are vigilant, partly because the reins of power are now shared between governments and those who are not governed by the ballot box yet have a huge influence on our lifestyles.

Examples are journalists, media moguls and the controllers of online platforms and they all carry a big responsibility for the way we think and act. Never let it be forgotten that those in power will do a lot, and some of them will do anything, to hold on to it.

Intolerance to disagreement

In western democracies, we have become complacent about our political leaders because we assume that when they no longer meet with our approval, we will remove them from power sooner or later. Sadly, we learn far too little from history or the experience of other cultures that this may not always be so. Not only in countries with little respect for democracy, but also perhaps, those who pride themselves on an open and fair system of government, the exercise of power and the way it transfers from one to another are being manipulated more and more.

Is it possible that we are losing the habit of open democracy of previous generations? Many more people than hitherto have recently become active in politics of which they approve, or intolerant of politics that they do not. This is true of almost every western democracy previously used to rubbing along as societies accepting a high level of internal agreement to disagree. People are more involved now than previously and not just those who habitually mount the barricades of protest. Whether it is populist phenomena or racist policing in the US, Brexit in Britain, gilets jaunes protests in France or the rise of the anti-immigrant far right in Germany, Hungary, Poland, Scandinavia, Benelux and others, politics has become a lot more vicious in the last half decade. Why is this?

It would not appear to emanate from real suffering. Over the last decade, there has no doubt been significant economic hardship imposed by austerity and the restriction of easy credit. However, no established democratic society has recently experienced anything remotely like, for example the mass hardships in Czarist Russia before the 1917 revolution, or Germany through the 1920s when the punitive terms of the Versailles Peace Treaty were beggaring the German economy. Yet the level of intolerance experienced recently about points of view other than one's own, is arguably similar to that of societies in Russia before 1917 or Germany through the 1920s and 1930s.

The symptoms of this intolerance are that too many of us have definite opinions about what we don't like, stick to those opinions rigidly, disbelieve evidence to the contrary and are willing to broadcast our preference in a range of media to suit. Ears are blocked and eyes too often closed to fresh data or evidence. 'Talk to the hand!' loud mouthing of a pre-fixed mantra of right or leftward tendency is the default response. Given that we are emphatically not living through the hardships of pre-revolutionary Russia or Weimar Germany, what is there to explain this intolerance?

The comfort of people like us
We have grown used to surrounding ourselves on a physical social scale with like-minded people, comfortably found among those doing largely similar jobs, living in similar areas or pursuing the same sorts of lifestyle. Ethnic similarity is too easily taken as a further symptom of people like us. Regardless of the richness that diversity would offer, we too often shun any variation to our social networks, to avoid the embarrassment of finding people with different fortunes in life whether better or worse, and thus contrasts in achievement or aspiration. Only on social media are we likely to encounter significant variations in lifestyle. And social media are not known for their tolerant behaviour and speech.

The result is a form of tribalisation of views and silo-ing of our mental dispositions from which they are formed. It is so much more comfortable to agree with the familiar than have to take issue with the unfamiliar. After all, it takes mental effort to justify a position which only in our deepest hearts do we know to be only partly formed. Any admission that the other person's point of view has merit is seen as an admission of one's own weakness.

Almost any political or social stance has to be filtered through the context of time and factors prevailing across social patterns during that era. A recent example is the heated issue of slavery from Africa to the Americas during the early years of European empire building in the fifteenth to eighteenth centuries. While the process was abhorrent by any standards and a deep stain on the morality of our ancestors, it is not sufficient to condemn it merely with a twenty-first century moral perspective. It also has to be seen for what it was at the time with eyes wide open to the values of the day – not just those of European slavers, but the African tribal leaders who collaborated with them to sell their people into captivity, disease and sometimes death for their own short term and cheap gain.

Such contextualising is not condoning. It does not make these crimes against humanity any less bad, but it enables us to understand how, as well as why, these things happened. I deliberately chose the highly emotive example of slavery the better to make the point. History is always contextual, and it is no good merely looking back at it through glasses tinted by our values of today. We do ourselves no favours by adopting high moral ground of current context, because out of that is borne the crimes of today as looked back upon sometime in the future.

Through providing historical context to events, we are able more easily to understand things better, amend our views or even change our minds when we gather fresh evidence. However, all too often, the default response to changing one's mind is denial. Perish the thought. It implies we had not got it all sorted out beforehand – an essential pre-requisite for those more concerned with self-image than authentically finding one's way through the intellectual minefield of conflicting points of view.

Is this a temporary period of polarisation of outlook or are we doomed to sit in our political and aspirational ghettoes for ever? Are we destined to rail against others with different views rather than seek them out with which to find at least accommodation or that rarest of intellectual gems – a change of mind? No matter that it is intelligent to change one's mind when the facts present themselves differently, flip-flopping as it is dismissively termed, is too often seen as weakness and a loss of personal judgement and integrity.

I spent a fair amount of the previous chapter looking at the impacts of social media and digital communications generally. So, there is no need to repeat any of that except where it impacts politics. There may have been a time when politics was something with which only the deeply committed were closely involved. Now that we live in a super-connected world with instant access to news and views on every subject, we are expected not only to have an opinion, but to stick to and broadcast it. When we discover that an opinion we hold, does not chime with those of others, we tend to disengage rather than talk the issues out.

I think this is all wrong and steering clear of difficult discussions about conflicting points of view only leads to the cementing in place of a fixed view. We need to find the confidence – in ourselves and others – to discuss differences and learn to embrace rather than shun them.

Learning civics – Whose side are you on?
At school from about the age of eleven or twelve, we had lessons in what was called civics. This was not on any exam curriculum

but was a way of introducing issues of the day and debating them. Despite our relative immaturity, we were deliberately asked to look at an issue outside of our mainstream concern from opposite points of view.

At the time, in early 1963, the vicious war of independence in Algeria, on which I elaborate in a later chapter, had recently ended and, to use Churchill's phrase, war-war had been replaced with jaw-jaw at what later became known as the Treaty of Evian. How would things be settled for the great majority of Algerians who supported independence, a minority who had supported French protection and, most complex of all, the so called pieds-noirs, French and other European colonists whose homes dating back a few generations would be displaced out of the North African littoral. Where were they to go?

We were given a few days to investigate the problem via the newspapers and current affairs programmes (*Tonight* with Cliff Michelmore and *Panorama* with Richard Dimbleby, in grainy black and white TV, I recall) and to prepare for a debate. We learned the alphabet soup of new organisations - OAS, FLN and so forth (and didn't dare mix them up). Our inclination as predominantly white European kids with similar events occurring in British or ex British colonial possessions, was to take the French side. But our civics teacher was nothing if not a challenger of received wisdoms and he set some of the brightest among us to argue the Algerian side. Some of the arguments must have demonstrated a lot of ignorance to those in the know, and some of it bordered on the childishly ludicrous (e.g. 'White people cannot take too much sun, so they should go home') despite the subject being anything but frivolous.

Halfway through the debate, the teacher sprung a surprise and the debating teams had to reverse sides. Those who had espoused France and ex French colonists (though in reality, these two were rapidly falling out with each other) had to swap shirts with the Algerians and argue for the other point of view. Those who had pitched for Algeria in the first round had some of their case hi-jacked by their opponents, quietly grateful for some supporting evidence of a cause they might otherwise have struggled with. There was also plenty of effort to outdo their opponents by ridiculous arguments. I recall General de Gaulle came in for quite a bit of stick as he seemed a ridiculous patrician figure to schoolboys.

Each side slowly realised they were playing team loyalty over and above the fundamentals of either case. Pretty soon, these being young boys with a limited attention span for serious politics, the debate became a contest in exchanging smart repartee rather than substantive arguments and the civics teacher closed it down. But his main lesson had been well learned; that there is always more than one point of view and you can only grasp any situation when it is contextualised. The pro Algerians won the day in a subsequent vote, partly because of the novelty and partly an English schoolboy inclination to tweak a French tail. None of this mattered much; our teacher – known for his pacifist views as a staunch Quaker who had served as a medal winning stretcher bearer in war – had deliberately chosen a subject outside our normal sphere of awareness, so as to reduce the risk of pre-conceptions. It was the presentation of opposing points of view that counted and the tacit acceptance that you could agree to disagree that emerged from having to make both cases.

With the Conservative government in disarray with sex, spy and leadership scandals throughout 1963, early the next year, we held a mock General Election anticipating the real thing that took place in October 1964. To everyone's surprise, in a fee-paying private school, the Labour Party won the day, and with a greater majority than the real one achieved later that year. This owed much to the charismatic thirteen-year-old Labour candidate who got everyone laughing about the ridiculous state the Tories had got themselves into and thanks to plenty of material which he had to work with. Even amongst young people barely entering their teens, it was easy to mock the Tories as a party not fit to govern. I recall, at the tender age of thirteen, the BBC's *That Was The Week That Was* became essential viewing during school holidays, as it had become for my parents. The cynical 1960s had arrived.

You can call this out as making light of serious issues, but the slow realisation in childhood that we needed to form opinions on current affairs seemed natural, but always to do so in an atmosphere of open debate. I am not sure that such a tradition of open discussion still prevails in many schools, partly because the exam curriculum now governs everything, leaving little time for debate for its own sake. But it may also be because of a sense that exposing differences might be a violation of individual free will. There seems to be a political correctness abroad these days that says, you are entitled to your opinions and I should not encroach on them with mine. I expect the same in· return. For me, this does nothing for the transparency required for people to fully air their views and help to form them via honest discussion. I hope it can change.

Finding the ends of the political rainbow

While at school, I was fascinated with how physical and thus, to an extent, social environments had such influence over people's party loyalties. In Britain in the 1960s, there really seemed to be only two tribes – Labour supporters from working class areas and Conservative supporters from middle class ones. They shared one thing in common – complete misunderstanding of each other to the extent that if you put a monkey up as the candidate and gave him a red rosette to wear in working class areas or a blue one in better off areas, he (it was almost always he) would get voted in. Quite a few party candidates seemed to fit that simian description. Personality or integrity of the candidate seemed less important than the colour of their party line and loyalty to it.

Despite this bi-polar pattern, business in politics seemed to be conducted more civilly than in recent times. Now people's political preferences and loyalties have changed. It is far more now a question of single issues that fire people up than a broad range of commonly held principles and aspirations otherwise known as an ideology. Thus, in the US, it is corrupt government and conniving politicians either red or blue (with no significant communist tradition, red denoting greater conservatism), while in the UK, it has been Brexit. In many countries, government management of the CV19 crisis will soon assume larger proportions of voter judgement than any other subject. No matter, I am not concerned just now, with the details of each of these issues but rather, the process of polarisation and separation into two armed camps and why this has occurred.

Immigrant pontoon: twist or stick
A lightning rod issue defining differences between these two-armed camps has been immigration. Always an underlying issue helping to define attitudes, immigration in the last two decades has risen to the top of the political agenda because of the massive increase in numbers of incomers involved. This has been fuelled within Europe by war, terrorism and unrest across adjacent land and sea borders with the Middle East and Africa. In the US, nearly identical trends have driven diasporas northwards from Central and South America, in similarly vast numbers.

It is easy to see from where social resentments have emerged and how those looking for single solutions first identify easy sources to blame. Scapegoat politics result, focusing on single solutions such as building walls to keep immigrants out, or throwing up tariff barriers to protect host population jobs. Stopping China and others from undercutting western technology and manufacturing has become a recent clarion call to unite people whose jobs and lifestyles appear threatened. Easy answers such as withdrawing from agencies designed to tackle such intergovernmental problems but deemed to have failed to do so such as UNESCO, the World Health Organisation or the European Union are proposed and implemented. It is argued that grievances have to be solved nationally these days, with much of the blame for the state we are in being put down to membership of international bodies. Let's just walk away – it's easier that way.

We now have a single word for this – populism. One of its successes has been the ability to personalize grievances but to have them expressed through collective voting intentions. But populism has happened before, albeit with slightly differing origins - but largely similar unpleasant outcomes. Previous manifestations might have fixed blame on Jews or Gypsies, while modern ones – in Europe at least - target Muslims. Immigration per se, does challenge host societies, but when tinged with xenophobia – justified by some as threats to host culture – it rapidly becomes toxic. A liberal and intellectual mindset believes immigration helps renew an often-ageing social demography, but it should also appreciate that for some, immigrants are a curse on employment prospects and a threat to host culture. These two points of view seem irreconcilable and as such, rarely meet to debate and find solutions that might identify a degree of shared benefit for all.

It is ironic that the often-maligned immigrants usually demonstrate this self-help bootstrap philosophy better than others. If you want something done, find an immigrant to do it! They are the ones with the get up and go, having already done just that at least once before. Larger cities provide the best seedbed for this enterprising culture despite their higher costs of living than elsewhere, higher living densities and often reduced physical quality of habitat. It is therefore ironic, that it is big cities where there is by and large least resentment of immigrants, contrasting with less metropolitan areas where immigrants are scarcer, yet where their presence is often resented more profoundly.

Resentment of incomers for stealing jobs, which might otherwise go to the indigenous population, generates grievance among what may be called the left-behinds. Such grievance leads to a loss of support for mainstream political parties offering one-nation social compacts. Faith in new solutions is instead, placed in parties offering single solutions to single problems - with no room for contextualizing. Between those with a populist view of the future and those believing in a more nuanced response based on the connectivity of all things, there is a massive gulf of misunderstanding. Never, has politics been so polarised. I look forward to the time when it becomes obvious that populist politicians are no more capable of solving the world's ills than those who espouse a more holistic approach.

I think we have to revert to the theme of my first chapter and say that the art of dialogue has progressively diminished to the point that it barely occurs outside of stage-managed broadcast debate. We keep our disagreements too much for the Internet where Twitter, Facebook and other media platforms are vehicles for abuse of those with whom we disagree. Instead, people are much happier going to meetings comprising monologue, the imparting of a message with which the vast majority are already in sympathy. We must push back against such balm for the soul rather than stimulation to the intellect.

These are not the values of diversity with which I and I hope, most fair-minded people, grew up and were educated.

What can we do about it? I don't mean what can we do to find agreement, but rather what can we do to return to a state of being prepared to disagree without abuse?

Living with difference

Am I just being nostalgic for a non-existent previous world where I merely imagine that people were civilised about their differences and comfortable living with them? There are plenty of examples from the individual and familial, right up to the national and international stage where disputes became toxic and people or governments cease talking to each other. I well remember my own youth when several contemporaries reported deep rifts with their families because of generational tensions, their insistence on being able to do their own thing and their parents being equally unbending in not allowing such under their own roof. Some of these led to long term family rifts and gaping emotional vacuums that everyone regretted but were too proud to admit. Not much live and let live there but now, we seem to do it at international level.

At the beginning of such political upheavals as the rise of Fascism in Italy or Nazism in Germany, there was a period where political debate was brutal and unyielding, only to be followed by worse; a long dark night of no debate at all as opponents of each regime kept their views to themselves in order to survive. Communism had no better record here, though a greater longevity of the silence occurred after the initial revolutionary upheavals, throughout which alternative views were suppressed to the point of near non-existence. In some countries, this still prevails.

Most of these trends were in a different and so far, a more tumultuous era. They were political patterns that pre-dated digital communication and its capacity for suppressing views from outside a party line via unattributed abuse, threats and trolling of fake news or negativity about those choosing to speak out. The earliest promoters of fake news were communist and fascist propaganda ministries set up to portray issues in a positive or negative light to suit the power brokers' view of what the mass opinion should be. They forced more open democratic societies to do the same and now everyone is at it.

A crusade for transparency in the forming of views
The ways out of this polarization are only long-term ones and they will take a generation of change by society. We have to build people's self confidence in community via more holistic education. Teaching civics again will be a critical part of this, not just to debate the issues of the day but to remind young people that we, meaning the whole world population, are a community – a realization that we are all in this together. There is no escaping that unless someone is planning a spaceship trip to other planets. And what might we discover there? Extra-terrestrial threats that might soon make us forget our small world differences back here on Earth perhaps.

We also need to re-build a pre-disposition to self-reliance so that greater numbers respond to the threats to their diminishing fortunes with flexibility, and a can-do attitude; a default reaction that says, "If governments will not or cannot help me, I will have to find the solution myself!" Some of this may appear to run counter to community focused thinking, because it calls on the individual to seek and act on solutions for him or herself. Understanding the congruence between self and collective obligations needs to be a constant theme of curriculum teaching across all educational levels.

There is now the opportunity for some pushback. Now, the power of the Internet and digital communication can be used by individuals for good as much as evil, by naming and shaming those intent on besmirching reputations or views which happen not to agree with those of the author. By pushing back against the trolls lurking there and waiting to besmirch and bully those with whom they disagree, the Internet could be a force for good as well as evil.

Why can we not devise unbreakable technology that requires all users of digital communication to have and display an identifiable and attributable signature? This would identify the source of all opinions both good and bad. It would clean up overnight some of the abuse, once you could only be heard if everyone knew who you were. For the trolls who invent fictional identities to hide behind false news or opinions damaging to their enemies, why can there not be a source code that fully identifies them? The right to an opinion should surely be qualified by the means to be identified for it and to be prepared to justify it to the public eye and ear. If we were all immediately identifiable, would we not be a little more circumspect about what we say online? Of course, we would.

We are all aware from where these problems emerged and from where we must look – and demand – for solutions to emerge - the FAANGs – Facebook (owning WhatsApp), Amazon, Apple, Netflix, and Google, and their Chinese equivalents of Huawei, ByteDance, Tencent, Weibo, and Baidu. The source technology of the companies that own these media platforms is understood and manipulated by many more agencies worldwide but it should not be beyond the wit and wisdom of international convention to impose regulation that only those who are fully identifiable can be allowed to post news and opinions. If this sounds like a charter for greater control over the way people think, consider the harm that is already being done by non-attributable news and opinions.

Truth is one of the most elusive qualities available to us, but in seeking to safeguard it, we have to start somewhere. The FAANGS and their Chinese and other equivalents will do for a starting point. These agents and promoters of technology say that it is not possible to fully attribute the source of messaging in any digital medium. They need to be challenged about this hiding behind the technology, by right-thinking agencies ranging from the narrowest individual through to the widest ones at civic and corporate level. The alternative is already here, and it is destroying social dialogue.

Left to itself, digital communication will take over our thoughts as effectively as Nazism, fascism and communism sought – but ultimately failed - to do. If there is a crusade to be joined just now, it is to persuade the FAANGs to abide by their duty to humanity's future and start imposing digital restrictions on abusive fake news and opinions. Get that right and perhaps, we can address the issue of encouraging future generations towards greater face-to-face dialogue, the stimulus of opposing argument and ultimately agreement to disagree.

Just now, the chances of identifying an international protocol to force identifiable digital signatures on every internet user are most unlikely to succeed. China and the US, as the two countries with the largest digital communication Apps are barely speaking to each other, let alone agreeing on issues of transparency of Internet communications. This atmosphere of almost complete bi-lateral mistrust is doing nothing for a more open and fairer digital communications world.

However, these solutions focus mainly on the medium not the message. We also need to re-develop our skills at formulating the message in the first place – building the evidence to generate sound judgements about the issues of the day. We can only achieve this effectively if we test partly formed opinions against those of others. Hearing evidence slightly contrary to our own might lead to a sharpening of the intellect, amending or strengthening of opinion or even a full-blown change of mind. This seems such a rare occurrence these days –

admission that one had got things wrong first time and thus to espouse a fresh viewpoint. Surely this is a strength rather than weakness.

No matter how judgements are formed, agreement to disagree is at the heart of understanding the power of dialogue and open debate. By re-introducing civics or current affairs into school curricula, we will be giving future generations the tools to formulate and understand both their own views and those of others. In arriving at opinions under the pressure of a formal syllabus, it might just mean greater respect for opposing views, because of the realisation that these were probably assembled in a similarly hit and miss manner to one's own. No one is perfect and the realisation of that in others, might just lead to more modesty about our own deficiencies. What could be a more conducive start to the pursuit of social harmony than that?

Chapter 3

Gender Wars from *Spare Rib* to #MeToo

Gender relations continue to evolve. What was acceptable behaviour five decades ago is not acceptable now. What is politically correct now will change again in the future. Love and mutual respect are just about the only immutable values that should endure, regardless of where any of us are coming from.

*

Gender relations are slowly evolving from the misogynistic and machismo past during which so many of us grew up without even noticing much of it. Here, we can have a look at what the genders really need from each other in public and private domains to build on changes for the better. There is still a long way to go.

This chapter is where, as a pale, male but hopefully not stale member of the human race, I venture into that minefield planted with more traps and explosive devices than many war zones, designed to catch the unwary writer navigating across uncharted space. That space is gender politics, not quite woke as in awareness of racism, though being woke about acceptable gender behaviour is rapidly becoming as nuanced as behaviour viz-a-viz race. It is also a generational thing, and for most people from mine – including me, as I am sure I am about to demonstrate - gender wokeness is hard to navigate. To start with, navigate in which direction? Most of those lost in minefields have some sense of where they need to go to get out of it. But which way for me to step, to avoid injury and is there any way out at all?

Whatever. Perhaps my mistakes will give greater reader pleasure than my convolutions to avoid offence. We all enjoy a little indignation at evidence of others' indiscretions – a form of schadenfreude rarely matched elsewhere in quasi-political discourse.

My quest in this chapter is to explore what has happened to gender behaviour over the last fifty years, and where might it be going. How can men and women communicate more effectively to nurture meaningful relationships and reduce the levels of tension that much of the media claim to be rife between the sexes? Let's see how effectively I can address these questions, and, as a baby boomer generation male, pass or fail the stringent but diametrically opposed tests of correctness as defined by closet misogynists and barricade-bestriding ultra-feminists. Most of us inhabit the space in between, but that will not absolve me from straying into their respective minefields. Here we go.

Political correctness rules, but I will speak my mind

I better qualify, if not obtain total absolution, by stating that I make no pretence in what I write to current political correctness. That concept is in a state of almost constant change anyway, thus defying any fixed-point definition, invariably rendered exclusive to each reader by his or her own standpoint. That is the whole point among misogynistic and ultra-feminist thinking. There is very little ground for agreement even among those of apparent like minds, revolution, and its step sibling counter revolution, having to be in a constant state of challenge and re-examination to remain relevant. Taking offence at other people's inability to express things in a woke way has become another way to be woke.

My way of defining the extremes of revolution and counter revolution will doubtless be called out as too male-focused. Rather than refer to misogynism, I could equally have defined the issue as misandrist (ingrained prejudice against men) and its implacable opponent male chauvinism, thus reversing my previous gender bias. But I can hardly attempt to present a case from a female perspective; I would probably be accused of gender appropriation. Better to be what you are, allowing others to point out your bias and correcting it with their own.

So, I plead guilty from the start to my male focus. That is the thing with gender wars, you are always open to attack for starting from the wrong standpoint. But I am not going to fall victim to that hidden explosive that assumes that the extremisms are merely equal opposites. Male chauvinism and misogyny are rarely out and proud these days, having to conduct their warfare from the undergrowth, while ultra-feminism and even misandry wave their flags from high places believing that they alone hold the moral compass. One definition of extremism might be anyone who thinks that the moral compass is their possession alone.

Feminism and me in the 1970s
My choice of chapter title reflects the first wide circulation feminist journal in the UK between 1972 and 1993. *Spare Rib* chose its title as a sarcastic reference to the Bible's Genesis Chap. II v. 22, where God is said to have taken a rib from his first creation Adam, to make his companion, Eve. I think we may assume that feminists and a good few others along with them were not literalists about the Bible. Metaphor and myth were profound themes in ancient storytelling, if only to retain intrigue among the campfire listeners. I doubt anyone has ever really believed the Genesis explanation of female bone structure or anatomy even from the time it was written.

But in 1972, *Spare Rib* was the ironic take on the secondary status from which feminists demanded the right to progress. Of course, feminism had been around long before 1972, but *Spare Rib* was, in the UK at any rate, its first mass media mouthpiece. It arrived about the same time as I was starting to take serious notice of such matters, the better to understand the opposite sex. The title and much of the early content caused quite a lot of controversy, yet it all seemed fair enough to me.

#MeToo kicked off in 2017 and is very much a second decade of the twenty-first century expression of feminism, and perhaps, a whole lot of other social trends at the same time. Some of its supporters would not even call themselves feminists; kick-arse self-awareness to call out bad male behaviour and build self-confidence might be more appropriate descriptions for some. Who could argue with that?

The #MeToo manifesto mainly revolves around resistance to the exploitation of the previously weak by the apparently strong, and the capacity, enhanced enormously by the internet, of calling out injustice, often around sexual harassment or worse but not exclusively. There are some very brave souls among the first of the movement. Invariably #MeToo focuses on exploitation of women by men, though I would not be surprised if there will soon be male chapters within #MeToo. But the forty-five intervening years between *Spare Rib* and #Me Too have seen much change - for men as well as women, and as #MeToo's arrival implies, not nearly enough. There may well be a way to go before a real sense of gender justice might prevail; gender parity may take a little longer.

I never understood the hostility that *Spare Rib* attracted when it first appeared on magazine shelves, especially from the ubiquitous nationwide magazine and bookseller at the time, WH Smith, who promptly banned it. Could they not see a rising trend and thus a major sales opportunity when it smacked them in the face? Apparently not, and they clearly did not want to offend their *Women's Weekly* or *Reader's Digest* following. The notoriety of their taking it off the shelves ensured the first edition sold out in days, suggesting a time-honoured principle that WH Smith just did not get – definitely not woke. So, beware of unintended consequences. WH Smith achieved the exact opposite of what they wanted – the oxygen of publicity.

Spare Rib's opponents may have regarded its message as driving a wedge between men and women and thus, as an attack on the natural order of the human species. "It's unnatural," I can still hear people say – including my own mother who was all in favour of women getting on and getting a fairer deal in life having been a pretty independent woman up to and after getting married in the middle of World War II and therefore, occupied with doing her bit. She did a lot then and later. But by 1972, and with the experience of young motherhood behind her, she had mellowed to a level of conservative thinking about gender equality, to appear to me to be a bit old-fashioned. She did, however, instil in me a respect for women that I only understood fully later when starting to observe examples of the disrespect handed out by some other men; creeps all of them.

The idea of upsetting a traditional order whereby men and women had established and separate roles in life was perhaps more profound than for a merely political philosophy. Personal and intimate balances about how things worked inside relationships were at stake here, and that made it all the harder for people – perhaps men more than women – to come to terms with an emerging new order. I recall understanding and occasionally, sympathising with, this traditional view; my position in the male dominant hierarchy in the non-domestic realm was being challenged after all. However, I could not help feeling that pure rejection of the feminist position was saying more about *Spare Rib's* opponents than it did about the feminists;

a whiff of excess sacrosanctity lurked around gender specific roles based purely on biology. For such opponents of the feminist agenda, social justice was fine, as long as it did not get in the way of biology. They seemed to be saying that cultural values could not be challenged as part of social evolution, a view I thought rather strange.

To me, excluding gender politics from the doleful list of the way some humans exploit others was part of the problem. But I was male and thus deemed by the more extreme female gender warriors as a net beneficiary of the privilege that men apparently enjoyed. So, I was unlikely to be invited to climb the barricades in support of a fairer deal for women while I climbed a greasy enough early career pole of my own.

I quite enjoyed reading some of *Spare Rib's* articles. I did not agree with some, but they were stimulus for thought, and I knew several girls who thought that it captured their stance on gender politics accurately. I lived in Bristol for five years after graduating in 1974 and *Spare Rib* was a very hot topic there with many of its contributors coming from the mean streets of St Paul's, as well as the more genteel purlieus of Clifton, Redland and Cotham. And though I did not agree with the outer fringes of their beliefs, I was attracted to girls that thought that way. Stay-at-home types seemed more boring and incurious by comparison. Remember that the sexiest part of a woman is her brain; men too, but what would I know?

Understandably, but inexcusably for the long-term success of its message, *Spare Rib* allowed a belief to grow that its protagonists and authors were man haters. This was probably never true and may have been promulgated by its more malign opponents, to ensure that thinking men did not join the cause. An early example of fake news perhaps? But *Spare Rib* even decided only to accept articles from men when there were no alternatives. Big mistake. I used to think that its message should be aimed at men at least as much as women. Both needed to change, but any opinion offered from a young male did seem to be met with suspicion by the feminist warriors. Too often, we men were said to be the enemy in the inaccurately titled war of the sexes, so while males should have been key targets for re-education, our views were not often listened to. Without a feminist publication also aimed at men, how were things going to change?

Revolutions are different for all; be careful what you wish for
All social movements evolve not at the behest of their principles but rather in response to events and the reactions to them of the movement's leaders. For most revolutions, it is principals not principles that really matter. The leadership is partly acknowledged by the followers but is partly self-appointed making up a lot of the rules as they go along. Interpretations of principles are different for everyone and we all have to compromise to some extent to accommodate random events and even our own inconsistencies of thought and action. As a result, like so many revolutions before and since, *Spare Rib's* main message of challenging the exploitation and de facto secondary status of women in relation to men, became diluted and pushed off course in various directions. This happened even though the purpose of correcting inequality should have been broadly beyond dispute for most right-thinking people.

Revolutionaries justify their tactics by saying that ends justify means and however painful is the shift from the current unacceptable status quo, those ends are worthwhile. Another interpretation of revolutionary philosophy states that you cannot risk being ignored, so that mould-breaking actions bring the oxygen of publicity whether good or bad, but they always attract attention. The former argument is pure iconoclasm, destruction of former belief at any price, while the latter is a more market-focused philosophy. Maybe the marketeers succeeded better because one of the more memorable trends of early *Spare Rib* promotions was the burning of bras. As a harmless example of good publicity, it served as much to titillate as to provoke deeper thought. Message dilution indeed, but after that, a lot of people lost sight of the serious underlying agenda.

There are few revolutions that have succeeded in achieving their original aims without inevitable compromise along the way. There is, however, a lot of alienation through compromise, of potential support that could have been expected by adopting a different approach. It is perception that counts in social politics because reality differs from one individual to the next.

Of course, everything is contextual. If I were to be writing about this topic as a female and perhaps of a different generation to my own, my perceptions of the *Spare Rib* movement would be quite different. More significantly, my point of view would be heard quite differently, because of who I am – a man, about whom militant feminists might too easily assume a variety of prejudices rendering my opinions predictable and therefore, easily dismissed with the response, "Well he would say that wouldn't he?" regardless of the validity, or otherwise, of what I am saying.

Both men and women have been engrossed in gender politics for decades - indeed centuries - whether they admit it or not, and most of the real wars of what might be defined as establishing the principles of egalitarianism were also being fought over long ago, usually with no lasting result; not much new in the world.

So, some complex issues here and perhaps, I need to set down my take on gender as the ways males and females interpret and act out their roles in society, homogenised as contrasting behaviours of two distinct categories of human being. Sex, meanwhile, may be defined as the determination of difference between male and female based purely on genitalia, what we do with them and how our brains determine and react to that.

Of course, this still falls far short of adequate coverage of all circumstances of gender interrelationships because such interpretation and acting out (as distinct from acting up) will invariably be wholly individual and sometimes deliberately cross gender. A small minority of females will always behave more like males and vice versa. That is okay, but I am not focusing my review of transition from *Spare Rib* to #MeToo on these - usually gay - minorities. They have as much right in an enlightened world, to behave as they see fit, provided it stops short of impinging on others, but I have little experience and no authority to offer opinions on gay rights or lifestyles. My subject is the majorities in both cases – heterosexual males and females and their gender-determined behaviours.

In my career lifetime, there have been big gender changes. Sex has moved on too, though probably not anatomically, as everything that might have been experimented on in recent decades, was probably tried long previously. There is little under the sun - or the sheets - that is new. But the gender changes we have experienced in the last fifty years are only milestones on a route that is much older, and we need to compare them with those occurring in previous centuries.

Men have not always dominated opposite sex relationships; many women would say that they never did, subject to how you define domination. Physical size and strength (as distinct to inner body resilience) has usually favoured men, but mentally and psychologically, women have probably had stronger influences over the male-female relationship as far back as anyone can remember or recorded.

For some men, that fact flies straight over their heads, part of why it is true. They just don't get it and strong women are often wise enough to leave their partners basking in ignorance.

This has led through the centuries to some aberrant behaviour; women who play down their influence on a partnership; and men who play out their woman's domination to the max, defining themselves as mere ciphers in the relationship when the truth is wholly different. There is also much in between and some of it out at the far ends of weird psycho - and sometimes sexual - distortion. I don't have much clue how to tackle those spectrum extremes, so, like my lack of authority about homosexuality, I will stick with the normal distribution curve of non-aberrant behaviours.

Are men or women ruling the world?

Around current affairs, politics and how history is recorded, it appears to have been a man's world since anyone can remember. It was men who fought most battles and got rewarded with medals for bravery or cursed with cowardice, wounds, or death for being the random victims of the unavoidable violence. War was and remains the inevitable consequence of disputes between tribes arguing over rights to hunt mammoths, through to whole nations and groups thereof settling existential differences of ideology or territorial possession. Only until very recently, was this predominantly a man thing.

It was mostly men who emerged as the leaders of tribes, communities and eventually nations, playing out the politics of wielding and retaining power by fair means or foul and often a nuanced combination of both. For most of history until recent times that included still-living witnesses, they did this partly by excluding women from the ruling process, on the dubious basis that women were a different species with entirely separate functions to perform usually restricted to family and community. Of course, there were exceptions as the occasional warrior women and many more examples of successful queens and leaders of countries demonstrates. But the principle of male dominance over decision and rulemaking for societies is long established and only recently subject to widespread challenge and change. Western democracies begrudgingly granted women universal suffrage slowly through the twentieth century. Women only assumed significant representative and leadership roles in government more recently still. Some countries applied universal suffrage only recently (e.g. Switzerland as recently as 1975) and many societies still deny women any say in social problem solving despite their intimate engagement in every aspect of society.

However, even at times of the most apparent dominance of men in the affairs of society, this was never the whole picture. Though it was the men who made sure their names were on the honour boards for bravery in war, the mayoral records, big treaties and the most impactful inventions, very often, they were far more reliant on the women in their lives than some of them cared to admit. This might have been seen purely as physical reliance – fed, watered, comforted domestically, gratified sexually etc, without even starting on the essential ingredients of tender love and care. But the psychology of this was still fundamental, recognised or not. The great advances of humankind would not have occurred without the women behind the men, despite the patronising tendency among some men to take all that for granted. Wise men acknowledged it whether quietly or otherwise.

Now things have changed because in a very wide range of cultures and societies whether democratic or autocratic, women are as likely to be in the forefront of team and other group leaderships, right up to the level of running whole countries and international organisations. There are two notable exceptions involving two large portions of the world's political cultures – Muslim societies and more surprisingly, communist ones.

For all its vaunted politics of female emancipation led by abortion and contraception policies in the Soviet Union after 1920, the way to the very top of Soviet communism remained effectively barred for women. And so, it has proved, when the revolution was exported. The few remaining self-professed communist states such as China and Vietnam, who anyway, now espouse capitalist economies of their own interpretation alongside left wing social controls, show few signs of advancing women in their political leaderships. Madame Mao comes to mind for her brief period of despotism following the longer one of her husband, the so-called Great Helmsman. But she probably only reached the position for that brief interval before her inevitable denouncement because of the longevity in power of the Chairman himself, however ruthless she proved to be in her own right. And ruthless she was.

Milka Planinc did preside over Yugoslavia in the early 1980s filling the vacuum left by the death of another long-serving leader, Joseph Tito. Even here, her contribution was all about the end of communist rule, and only a few years later, the breaking up of Yugoslavia altogether. Brave woman, tragic consequences.

Otherwise, I struggled to find a communist country anywhere led by a woman, an extraordinary negative for a social philosophy that proclaimed casting off the shackles of exploitation by the few of the many. Not so for the female half of the proletariat perhaps? Communism could be remarkably conservative in its twilight years.

Muslim countries continue to be the single racial, cultural, or religious group where women commonly play a far less significant role than men at the level of state politics. There are some partial exceptions such as Oman, neighbour to the most male-oriented society of all in Saudi Arabia, but such exceptions broadly emphasise the rule. Traditional Muslim clerics cite the Koran as the wellspring of this, but in reading it to the extent of using an invaluable cross reference index, I have not found any specific references to women as second-class citizens. More likely the gradual subservience of women to men in the most traditional Muslim societies is historical and cultural rather than theological. I address this further in my later chapter on trauma.

These two populous exceptions apart, anyone in politics seen to be openly resisting the widespread advance of women towards political power is now widely seen as a social dinosaur. Such gender re-balances of power at the level of statehood, remain the exception not the rule because fixed patterns of male domination take time to change. But now, few express surprise when women are in charge – novelty perhaps but not surprise. The social trajectory is for this to continue and I for one, am excited by that prospect. Those women finding themselves in positions of power are as likely to be supported by men who have slipped into a supporting role seamlessly, a fact probably insufficiently acknowledged by either gender.

Yet, how recent has been this change. The female prime ministers or elected presidents of countries, such as Golda Meier in Israel, Indira Gandi in India, Benazir Bhutto in Pakistan, Sirimovo Bandaranaike in Ceylon (which became Sri Lanka on her watch), Michelle Bachelet in Chile, Christina Fernandez Kirchner in Argentina, Vigdis Finnbogadottir in Iceland, Gro Harlem Bruntlandt in Norway, Julia Timoshenko in Ukraine, Margaret Thatcher and Theresa May in the UK, Angela Merkel in Germany, Julia Gillard in Australia and most recently, Jacinda Ardern in New Zealand, have all led their countries during my lifetime. Apart from monarchs who gained their ascendancy through inheritance rather than leadership, I can think of none who preceded them electorally. These fourteen women leaders have shown themselves as capable or incompetent – and sometimes ruthlessly single-minded or vacillating – as the men who preceded or have followed them since.

Despite the short list, there might now be just sufficient female elected leaders across varied political and social cultures to draw out some conclusions about their performance. For those who expected that women would be incapable of making the tough decisions incumbent on political leaders, there is no clear evidence. Are they necessarily more consensual and less bellicose than men? Not really. Several of those I listed have taken the fateful step of declaring war on their countries' enemies (Meir, Thatcher) while others have declared states of civil or financial emergency that proved draconian for some of their citizens (Gandi, Bhutto, Kirchner and Tymoshenko). Others were implicated directly or indirectly and rightly or wrongly in corruption scandals related to abuses while they were in power (Bhutto, Bachelet, Kirchner and Tymoshenko).

Meanwhile, for those who expected women to be more sensitive to social or economic impacts of their policies and thus to be inclined to adopt consensual measures to compensate, or merely to be indecisive, again there is no clear evidence. Indeed, there is plenty of evidence to the contrary (e.g. Thatcher on closure of coal pits, Merkel – eventually - on immigration). Some promoted the advancement of other women in their governments, (Bruntlandt and Finnbogadottir) but others who were indifferent to such positive discrimination measures, felt that the advance of another woman's career was that woman's responsibility alone. They may have actively suppressed other women's advance in their own power bases regarding them as a threat to their own unique power (Thatcher, Kirchner, Bandaranaike, Bhutto, Gandi and perhaps others.) But who can really tell? Such personal histories will invariably be interpreted to suit the preconceptions of the observer.

The only conclusion I can draw from the performance of women as political leaders compared to men is that their gender was simply not an issue. They have proved to date at any rate, no better nor worse than their male colleagues. In what statisticians would define as a zero correlation, gender has in my view, proved insignificant as regards quality of performance in national leadership. But the statistical base is still small, and I left out Ardern from the above review. Her legacy is still evolving but she has demonstrated high leadership qualities over terrorism in Christchurch and most recently the handling of the CV19 crisis in her country.

One thing is shared by them all - selective misogynism about their being leaders in the first place. It is one thing to call out a leader for not being a strong enough leader, but another and unacceptable, in my view, to add the underlying criticism that their performance owes much to their gender. No one knows this more than Julia Gillard in Australia who was the victim of some of the worst chauvinism imaginable that outed itself alongside some more justifiable criticism of her performance as prime minister. Her 'Ditch the Witch' speech in the Canberra Parliament in 2010 nailed some of the worst of this behaviour. Pity that her eloquence on the issue of misogyny could not translate more effectively into good governance.

How much influence are women getting in running business?
How does national politics compare with business, commerce and the regular employment market? There are now few publicly listed companies who would dare not have female representation on their boards, though there is a long way to go to achieve anything approaching numerical parity. I believe that women will have had to be a lot better than men to get there,

though there is always the sneaky suspicion, probably more false than true, that some underperformers have been shoe-ins to make up numbers. There are equally plenty of men on company boards who have achieved their positions more through longevity of service than real competence.

It is typical of the tail end of any lingering trend of exploitation: that those representing the new wave are merely the contributors to a numbers game rather than super performers in their own right. There are bound to be representatives of both in any senior board appointments but I suspect that like national leadership, there will be no major difference in the longer term as regards female managerial performance in business compared with their male equivalents.

However, company boards will be much better off whether or not the women match or exceed their male colleagues for competent corporate governance, if only because they provide a better balance to the decision processes. In companies with a proper grasp of their mission to the wider stakeholder community rather than merely their shareholders, there are far too many consequences of any major corporate decision to exclude a female point of view. Actively to encourage those viewpoints to drive and lead board decision-making has got to be an improvement on the past. Senior appointments will eventually become gender blind and that is how it should be for a more representative corporate world. One consequence of the recent pandemic must surely be the swifter realisation of that more representative corporate world.

I sat alongside women on company boards, but I am probably a member of the last generation of men for whom it will be common to say that I never had a female boss. Many men say (usually quietly, if they are wise) that they would have dreaded having a female boss, but I think I would have enjoyed the experience – a new challenge for the mind. Thinking back through many projects and different roles I have played, the bosses I admired were never the macho types. On the contrary, the best were usually the better listeners. If women have a reputation for being better at listening to people (I have no evidence of any universal application) then they would have been good bosses as far as I am concerned. But their gender would almost certainly have been irrelevant.

My professional sectors of urban master planning and development surveying are still male dominated, but town planning less and less. There have now been numerous female presidents of our professional institute and like their sisters in national government, they seem to have performed broadly similar to men. Again, gender does not seem to be an issue.

Turning to the regular employment market, the under-rewarding of women in relation to men continues, but the discrepancies are now steadily narrowing. There are countless good references to demonstrate this from which I chose an excellent American website payscale.com Using a very large sample size enabled through its client base that includes Amazon, the New York Times and Washington Post, it demonstrates that for every dollar earned by men, women in the US earned seventy-four cents in 2015, but that this had improved to eighty-one cents by 2020. This represents a nine per cent improvement over five years that would see women achieve pay parity in little over ten more years.

I can already hear from the barricades that such disparity should never have been allowed to exist and the rate of correction is far too slow. Of course, those views are right. The website also quotes the highly rated Pew Research Centre that forty-two per cent of women have experienced discrimination (real, not imagined I am assuming) in the workplace compared with twenty per cent of men. That pay gap must be one such measure of discrimination, so I believe those statistics. Most women, including the great majority who do not sit on the barricades of the feminist revolution, would accept that pay gaps and discrimination can only shrink with time. What enrages them, rightly in my view, are those men (and a very few women) who deny the differences or make light of them for a variety of prejudicial reasons such as the so-called motherhood penalty. I am prepared to believe overwhelming empirical evidence not only of the injustices of women's widespread discrimination at work, but also the slow yet steady erosion of these unacceptable trends.

What about sex?

What about another extreme of the gender power spectrum – sex? Loving relationships including sex are probably definable by the absence of exploitation. But where sex has been transactional, the main beneficiary through the centuries has been the male of the species with women invariably the exploited party. It is true that women in positions of power have always, like powerful men, been able to exploit the opposite sex for sexual favours, but the common denominator here has been the exercise of that power rather than the sexual gratification itself. As women assume greater influence over public affairs, whether in the political or commercial realms, so their capacity and appetite for exploiting men - and other women of course – purely for sex may grow. It is the power thing that will drive it.

So, we arrive at the original wellspring for the #MeToo movement. This successor to *Spare Rib* has been more, "Hell no, we won't put up with this any longer!" than any evolution of a political philosophy. We have seen, in recent years, various documentaries charting the course of male exploiters of females for sexual favours. This phenomenon of exposure is probably unique in history because of the near impossibility prior to our digital and broadcasting age to assemble so much evidence in one place. It reveals the ugly side of power relations that reflect badly on the exploiters and have led in some cases to their suicides or death by another hand. Few will have mourned the loss of such monsters from society whose former influence is insufficiently redressed by their falls from grace. The vanity which invariably accompanied such exercise of power will have sat uneasily with its loss and the resultant private hell might be making up for some of the injustice felt by the victims and wider society.

To what extent is #MeToo a true successor to *Spare Rib? Spare Rib* was a mouthpiece to a mass movement, reflecting a widespread social trend. Meanwhile, #MeToo started as a victim support group that evolved into a cry of rage from many whose exploitation may not have reached the depths experienced by its worst victims, but who recognised the circumstances and incipient power broking that preceded the acts themselves. To the extent that sex is the ultimate carnal expression of male-female interaction, challenging some of the exploitative ways it occurs, will always be difficult. I am not sure that, on its own, #MeToo can sufficiently replace a broad social drive for greater equality of opportunity across all life experience.

One thing seems certain: any transactional compact purely for sex starts to break down when empathy and meaningful connection is introduced to the relationship. It seems to me that when the most intimate of human relations is involved, it can only work between strangers based on minimal psychological connection between them. Anything further by way of a spark of recognition that each party is a human being seeking to relate to the other, is bound to complicate things and threatens the purely transactional nature of physical gratification. Perhaps it is simply true that empathy and sex will only mix where love and thus mutual respect is also present. What a traditional conclusion, but hardly surprising perhaps as it owes its survival to the test of time.

I can only assume that the progressive advance of a more liberated society will see the parallel advance in the number of establishments offering women de-personalised sexual gratification from men. Of course, for the last two decades and perhaps more, this sort of trade has become well established online and thus ostensibly in greater privacy, thus offering the option of house calls and not actually visiting an establishment set up for the purpose. The object of temporary desire can be commissioned online to come to the customer (at some greater risk to both) but reversing a previous trend that the customer usually had to go to the source of gratification. Technology is changing the deal.

It is a fact that most men and women adhere to gender defined differences in the way and pace that they become sexually aroused. But this will not slow the advance of establishments, on or offline, that cater predominantly to women customers. As observed in my first chapter, we are now living in a short-term gratification society and that holds good for women as much as for men. The idea of the quick knee trembler probably now has as much resonance for females as well as males, either that or it was always thus but no one cared to admit it. In this way, the two sexes are not much different.

Objectification or empowerment: the real battle front

The real change that I see in gender politics is no longer to do with greater liberation for women as that continues gradually to improve, but the battle between empowerment and objectification. This is a subtle variation on the equality issue per se that has been the main battleground for decades. Many of the latest generation of feminists would probably ask, "Equal to whom?" My impression is that they have moved on and are no longer concerned with equality with men but empowerment as women alone – to achieve for themselves what they want and not be restricted by a paucity of ambition either self-induced or imposed by others. It is almost as if women are a different species to men, and to some extent, I see where that opinion is coming from. I think this might be one of the prime if unspoken, differences between #MeToo and pure feminism from the past. #MeToo would seem to derive strength in its attitude to fighting back against exploitation, possibly in the end genderless, despite the sad predominance of females among its victims. But it is also far more self-absorbed than the collectivist spirit that inspired *Spare Rib* in the seventies. To that extent, they are true reflections of the centuries in which they were formed.

A lot of the empowerment now sought is a push back against men's attitudes and quite rightly so where these are predatory or otherwise negative towards women. Hence, the choice of the term objectification, because that is at the heart of the wrong that some men still inflict on women – identification of women as subservient partners, domestic slaves, sex objects or merely 'sex opportunities'. I may have got this wrong but this to me, is the heart of the motivation for the #MeToo movement, to call out where men are reducing women to something other than equal partners in society via sexual harassment or sexual assault.

Am I alone in failing to understand why some men behave as predators towards women? Maybe my sex drive is not as acute as that of the predators, but if their objective is sexual gratification, they seem to be going about it entirely the wrong way! As a means of attracting women or gaining their positive attention, predatory behaviour is one hundred per cent guaranteed to fail. If the sole objective is to dominate women either physically or mentally, it is going to fail with the ninety-nine per cent of females who are motivated by a more balanced relationship. Exploitation, as we are discovering while the more lurid and persistent cases get documented by the brave victims, is less to do with sex and more to do with the exercise of power. Again, I struggle to understand, because the ultimate expression of power is not having to use or demonstrate it. So, any overt display of apparent domination becomes its opposite – an expression of weakness and inadequacy.

This gradual evolution from objectification to empowering women towards greater equality is sadly a long way from realisation in many cultures. In numerous eastern societies, including countries otherwise sophisticated in terms of material wealth at the personal scale, prostitution is still an enormous part of the culture and even the tourist industry. For example, in Thailand, it has been estimated by Dr. Nitet Tinnakul at Chulalongkorn University that as many as 2.8 million people worked in the Thai sex industry in 2003, the great majority being women of whom eight-hundred thousand might have been less than eighteen years old. An update of such research is much needed approaching twenty years later, but the Thai government seems reluctant to encourage further investigation reflecting negatively on concern for their people.

Patpong in Bangkok, Pattaya Beach and Phuket are said to be the main centres of this industry and though prostitution has been technically illegal (subject to some ambiguous conditions) since 1996, it remains widespread. I first visited Bangkok on business, in 1996 including an almost obligatory drinking tour of the Patpong District with local clients. The so-called girlie bars were a mix of light entertainment (girls revolving round steel poles) and heavy petting in public (back massages with your shirt on) that could easily escalate for those so inclined via one to one encounters elsewhere in each establishment. I chose not to escalate having adopted the principle of look but don't touch. The atmosphere was superficially macho but close observation of the (mostly foreign) men ogling the photogenic girls, suggested that the males were in obsessional visual thrall to the females. I am not sure where the power lay in the room, but it was certainly not with the customers. Probably not the girls either, as there remained no shortage of supply to meet the demand.

To suggest that there is change afoot from objectification to empowerment in such societies is clearly wide of the mark and it will take years to change. Ultimately the contrasts between east and west in this case, boil down to a different value placed on quality of life, driven by the motivation to break out of poverty and earning money fast. Narrowing the difference between the relative wealth of the customers in Patpong and places like it, and those offering the sex services, remains a long-term endeavour.

The moderation of vox pop
My views on these issues count for little of course without gaining the views of women of various ages and backgrounds. A useful objective would be to see where they stand on the spectrum of opinions from quiet acquiescence of current status quo in gender relations to standing on the barricades of an active gender revolution. To that end, I recently conducted a vox pop of women not selected by me but by my wife's hairdresser. While I readily and rapidly admit to this as utterly unscientific, based as it is, on the geographical specific of a mixed community in Fulham west London, it had certain merits to recommend it. So what if my survey contains geographical or social bias? They were opinions nonetheless and to my pleasant surprise, I received them in droves.

I had composed a written questionnaire seeking views on how respondents thought opportunities for women had developed over the last thirty years. The questions included how the respondents considered relationships with men had evolved over the same period. The form would have taken between five to ten minutes to complete and while I identified myself by name, as an author seeking opinions for a chapter on the subject in a book about empathy and human connectivity, the respondents did not have to speak to me face-to-face. I thought this would yield more frank and honest responses while the environment of a hairdressing salon offered a fair bit of time available not to rush written answers. That much at least, is reflected in the thoughtfulness of what I received back.

Under the study title of *Better Understanding of a Woman's Perspective*, here were the questions I asked.

1. *Do you think women get more realistic choices of career opportunities than thirty years ago?*
2. *If yes, what has changed? e.g.*
   - *Wider educational range of qualifying subjects at school?*
   - *Better careers advice and expectations?*
   - *Changing attitudes among (mainly male) employers?*
   - *Women demanding and getting fairer consideration as candidates for different careers?*
   - *Anything else?*
3. *If no, what needs to change?*
   - *Any of the above answers to Q2?*
   - *Other (please specify).*
4. *Do you think women get more respect from men than thirty years ago?*
5. *How have relations between men and women changed in the last thirty years?*
6. *Do you think gender politics have improved in the last thirty years?*
   - *If yes, in what ways?*
   - *If no, why, and what might be done to improve things?*

I would ask one further thing from you, to help categorize the answers. Not your age, (of course!) but the approximate time you were born;
- *Before 1964 (Baby boomers)*
- *1964 to 1980 (Generation X – for some reason)*
- *1980 to 2000 (Millennials)*
- *After 2000 (Generation Z – (don't blame me for these titles, blame the sociologists)*
Any further comments you would like to add:-

I had few illusions about getting any significant results from this, but the female assistants in the busy hairdressing salon were very eager to help, once they understood what I was trying to obtain. They drove the idea with as much, if not more enthusiasm, than me. Over the course of several weeks, they subjected their customers to some initial hairdresser chat about gender politics before suggesting gently that the completion of a questionnaire on the subject would give the opportunity to express views more openly. A surprisingly large number agreed to take part and the results were revealing.

It seemed as if I had tapped a wellspring of opinions. Because of the way the questionnaire was formatted, these came out pretty much as each respondent chose, but they were instructive. Answers rapidly departed from my chosen question structure probably saying more about the desire to express opinions than to my skill at designing an opinion survey.

Here were the more thought-provoking issues raised:

1.   Men from older generations are stuck in their ways and would not change their attitudes to women unless they were forced to by legislation or women's more assertive attitudes. But boys now grow up seeing girls differently to

previous generations. They are more accepting of girls being equal to them.

2.   Some women still like to be 'pampered' by men, but such women are looked down on as old-fashioned by the younger generation. This has led to a loss of kindness between the sexes and generations.

3.   The broader educational range of career options for women has done much to improve expectations and achievements. Schools are critical to continuing this change in attitudes – as important for boys as it is for girls.

4.   Girls still predominate in (so called) caring careers such as nursing and teaching, but it is changing. More are pursuing careers in engineering and politics, professions that used to be male dominated environments, but it is tough.

5.   There remains a long way to go to achieve true equality and women are going to have to continue as the main drivers of this.

6.   Older respondents expressed envy at the opportunities for girls nowadays wishing they could have their lives over to do things differently.

Despite the salon catering for a lot of younger women, there was a singular absence of barricades-style feminism in the replies. This was surprising given the ample scope for anonymity or even a platform for broadcasting trenchant views. Overall, I found the opinions expressed to be predominantly mainstream, but those first and last listed above were the most thought-provoking. Changing attitudes among males to which replies to the first question refer, can only grow as Neanderthal males of my generation die off. Despite the recourse to legislation expressed by many respondents as the only route to greater equality, it is also this sea change in male opinion that will ensure profound and lasting change.

The last observation was also a significant view from across a wide number of replies implying that it was without generational bias - the envy expressed by older women for the opportunities now available to girls entering adulthood. I felt this poignant absence of opportunity not only for the individuals, perhaps of my generation, who replied, but also for society as a whole for the absence of social, technological and economic change that might otherwise have been achieved had previous female generations been given the career opportunities now becoming available. The world has forsaken so much career realisable talent, simply because of prejudices, expectations and the blunting of aspiration. Younger sisters among this admittedly un-scientific demographic, had better step up to the challenge from their elders as much as the boys and men gradually making way for them.

Love and respect are the keys; like always

Gender interplay will continue to dominate our day-to-day lives. Why not? A lot of it is fun. But it is such a different gender world that I now inhabit to the one in which I grew up. Anyone of any great age mouths this truism, but what we always find difficult is to portray to younger folk what it was like living with received wisdoms of earlier times. Applying the mores of the present to past behaviour patterns distorts things and is all too easy. It also displays ignorance. There may have been much wrong, but it is facile merely to criticise the way things were. Contextualizing is not condoning. The great majority of us males of former generations, travelled alongside the worst excesses of female exploitation without being aware of it taking place and hopefully, not taking part. We were not its perpetrators. We may not have been the fully free thinkers challenging the status quo, but most men still treated women with more respect than is often now portrayed.

Though I admire those seeking to break moulds, partly because they saw the injustices before I did, I am also aware that their fight may have distorted their outlook. Revolutions rarely end up where the activists want, their contrarian natures see to that as much as the random way social change plays out. But I see no great change in two abiding values between the sexes on either side of the great divide across which we stare sometimes uncomprehendingly at each other. Love and mutual respect will ensure a happy long-term future between the genders for the great majority of us. About that I am certain, because I am a human first, before being a man. Once again, as for so much else in the prejudicial world of human relations, mutual respect is the key to future solutions.

Chapter 4

Office Interactions

A typical office environment forty years ago was a lot more red-blooded than now! Recent changes to how we do our work have created an environment where people feel increasingly isolated. The rise in working from home and communicating with colleagues through digital devices, accelerated by CV19, is steadily removing the benefits of building work relationships face-to-face.

*

In post-industrial economies, the office has steadily become the commonest indoor environment most of us experience outside the home. Until CV19 struck, we spent eight-hour days and often a lot more there, while even the most ardent shopaholics have had enough retail therapy after three or four hours before retiring for their skinny lattes or chokka mokkas. In recent months, that has been challenged fundamentally through the need to isolate or maintain social distance and, to the surprise of many bosses, the idea of working from home with frequent recourse to digital meetings, has worked surprisingly well. Managers of business will be compelled to re-consider whether maintaining office space for an entire workforce is necessary with rents comprising one of the largest single business costs most companies have to contend with. Reductions in office space provision will change the dynamics of town centres fundamentally, but my main concern here is how has it influenced the way things were in team building, generating a common purpose in delivering projects, and how that might all change in the future.

Office space has changed subtly but radically through my career lifetime. What I experienced when starting out in the mid-seventies would not now be recognised anywhere, and the changes have probably been common to all service sectors of the economy. How do I see these changes impacting our relationships with fellow workers?

There was still, in the mid-seventies, a hierarchy based on function and seniority and you learned to toe-the-line swiftly, not to put either foot wrong across it. Not much different now I hear you thinking. But the difference in the seventies was that these hierarchies were expressed spatially as well as psychologically – in a way that has substantially disappeared since. It was outwardly relaxed, the freewheeling sixties had seen to that, but people still jealously guarded their privileges. Space and status were power.

Divisions of labour

First off, there was much more division of labour, not to mention gender, prior to the personal computer age. In the offices that I inhabited, predominantly male teams of young architects, engineers and town planners might write or type their reports and memos, but a female dominant typing pool turned them into formatted text and layout. Your work entered a queuing system, the absence of human contact within which, either required acceptance of the long delays as a member of the lowly-ranked, or if you were prepared to risk it, application of buttery charm through the cigarette smoke to get things done a bit faster. Within the intimidating typing pool, there was a rich vein of psycho-sexual innuendo that would be off the scale of political correctness nowadays. Most of this was female-on-male. Recent graduates were fresh bait for the long-serving and suffering queens of the pool whose backchat often demanded every form of imagined favour in return for a fast report turnaround. Their messages of doom were delivered in gravelly heavy smoker voices, "You want your work back, when? This afternoon? Well dearie, that will depend on what you're offering me!" It was all innuendo to relieve the boredom of typing drudgery but if you did not play along, you were quickly branded as humourless, stuck up or worse, and your purple prose would languish at the bottom of the in-tray.

Woe betide anyone making radical edits to their text after typing. Out would come the paper, scissors and Tippex bottle with threats for them to be applied gleefully or with mock dread to sensitive parts of the male anatomy. For bigger editorials imposed by the boss's pen (green ink, I recall), a whole re-type was inevitable, at the cost of theatrical sighs and eye rolling, endured by the original author with a mixture of sweet tolerance and grovelling apology. Blame it on the boss, but sarcasm or irony was only a conversational option for the long-suffering typists. They had seen it all before and they commanded the uplands of functional superiority, "We do our job as best we can, but you clearly need to do yours better!"

Painfully through the nineties and into this century, I, like millions of others, learned to word process my own reports, usually acquiring every trick of the Microsoft software and its early painful lack of intuitiveness, doing it the hard way – trial and error. The days of the typing pool and their real or imagined pantomime characters were soon gone and with them, some of the colour that made offices fun and unique to themselves.

Memos were a leisurely and better-considered exchange of views in the seventies, slowly replaced with multiple email now. This now amounts to verbal ping-pong, winging back and forth through cyberspace every day, sometimes with little visible progress on any material issues raised. But in the seventies, for anything outside of one's own department, memos travelled via the post room and thence externally, via courier or the Royal Mail. Often, overseas material came back faster using the Telex, than that sent to another office at home, but this still relied on yet another department, named Comms, in charge of the complex electronics including the remote, security protected, air-conditioned reel-to-reel computer drives of the day; a.k.a. 'Join the telex operator queue!' Why memos, not phone calls? Because like email today, the main audience was frequently not the original correspondent but some of those copied in, including the boss, who was supposed to be impressed by the clarity of thought by which you were solving this latest technical or political hurdle.

The print room was another (semi-industrial and thus unionised) environment where charm skills like those applied in the typing pool were needed. The only variant was gender. This was a strictly male-only environment such that only grossly misogynistic remarks were permitted. To get your urgent report back in anything under a week, printed and bound and thus, ready for dispatch to an impatient overseas client, a subtly different form of banter was called for. The typing pool and print room came together once a year for the Christmas party, with consequent attendant fireworks. They were fun to watch once some of us had applied some mild ignition and conversational lighter fuel.

Our business was planning and design consultancy across architecture, engineering and town planning, usually working internationally from the UK. So, for the many projects overseas in often obscure locations, there was the special preparatory joy of a visit to the travel department to dispatch or receive courier packaged reports and plans. All this preceded the client visit and thence, the airline tickets and visas for the fact-finding trip. Scope for wangling upgrades on long haul flights required a fertile mind and more of the buttery charm not already exhausted on the typing pool. But this was face-to-face haggling not via an impenetrable online booking system. You could work the system a bit to enable you to 'turn left, not right' when entering the plane if you were a regular flyer. Security seemed a distant consideration as airside terrorism was then only in its early hijacking phase. Aircraft also had more legroom back then and less in-flight rage. It all seemed a bit more civilised; some even wore a jacket and tie in hope of winning those upgrades.

Divisions of space

Heads of department inhabited enclosed office space, entry to which was guarded fiercely by their secretaries, only then being granted a modicum of egalitarianism with the new title, PA. If you had an important point to make and wanted to be noticed for advancement up the greasy pole, focus on the secretary not the boss. She (it was always she) controlled access and often the opinions of His (it was invariably His) Majesty. Again, depending on age, demeanour and disposition of this gatekeeper, charm, seriousness, professional competence, or the occasional levity needed applying liberally to get one's point across. Flirting with the PA was off the agenda. And it was no good just sitting in your booth, hoping to be noticed. If you did not stand out, someone else would. A mixture of gravitas and insouciance were my usual choice of ingredients, but I tried applying some spicy humour as well, to ginger up the recipe if the occasion suggested it. It did not always work.

The office cafeteria with its lunch breaks away from your desk strongly encouraged, and the ubiquitous tea lady, subject of so many TV and radio sitcoms through the sixties and early seventies, completed the line-up of regular office dramatis personae. The tea lady had usually been with the firm for thirty years and had a special retainer-style relationship with the chairman. So, she could not be messed with. She had carte blanche to access all office space at any time. Who would be without their morning tea or coffee break, and if you were lucky, chocolate digestives?

I sometimes think the tea ladies exercised their mesmeric power over the most senior of directors for the sake of a chocolate digestive. Empires were won and lost on less. Interrupting the highest levels of time-pressed meetings, they would write down their slow inventory of personal beverage preferences either to familiar but tolerant exchanges of banter, or when unfamiliar clients were present, in sepulchral silence. The ritual took just as long, whoever was present. It did not do to hurry or shoo her out from even the most important meetings with pressing business to get through. A kind of grace and favour atmosphere existed affording the bosses the opportunity to display their democratic credentials to the lowliest office staff and foreign dignitaries. "Everyone counts in our culture. Look how kindly I deal with the tea lady," was the subliminal message. Foreign dignitaries just looked completely baffled by this ritual, but the oh-so-British tradition of personally served warm beverages was a sacrosanct and distant echo of a bygone age. Like so much else, this and others have now long gone.

This separation of function afforded time between our technical or procedural deliberations for further endless banter around the office, the metaphorical sugar in a sometimes, tasteless tea, coffee and milk substitute. A sense of progress seemed slower than today, though I am not sure that productivity was quite so far behind. Time still represented money, but this was time to reflect - on complex professional issues such as the client brief, design parameters and problem solving, decision sequences for consenting of new development, environmental or social impacts of our proposals and the like. These vital ingredients of a good urban master plan now get too short shrift in the demanding atmosphere of being seen to reply instantly, if not resolve each problem as it comes up. Today's emails rarely resolve problems that quickly, by merely circulating them more than once. They are ping-pong not table tennis.

The march of digital technology

Things started to shift with universal computer use as we transitioned from painfully acquired FORTRAN through big beige Amstrad desktops and beneath-the-desk disk drives using clunky word processing and spreadsheet data handling systems, to the halcyon modern era with its widespread use of portable laptops and their MS software. I struggle now to remember what it was like before say 1990, by which time email was no longer regularly crashing from capacity overload and everyone was expected, as now, to do everything for themselves.

In the seventies, we were experiencing the back of a wave of individuality that had hit Britain like a social thunderclap during the 1960s. One metaphor for this was the *Beatles* whose sense of togetherness in the sixties was the taproot of their brilliant composing. Most pop music was happy-go-lucky then as they led us through their Strawberry Fields forever. By the 1970s, the *Beatles* had broken up to our near universal regret and their two best composers and writers, John and Paul were going their separate ways. The flavour of their song-writing often matched the growing bolshiness in society - defiance of authority not through a summer of love style, but an 'I'm not taking any more shit from you', type of interaction.

We were pretty conventional types in our professional office, not wishing to behave too much like rebels having invested too much education and qualifying time (five or six years in undergraduate and post graduate university, in most cases) to ruin our nascent careers. However, we still railed against autocratic authority and were ready to call it out.

Failing to toe-the-line

There was once a boss in our office (let me call him the autocrat) who had been brought in to sharpen up our cost control. And not just our excessive use of stationery but to tackle the largest single currency of our trade - time taken to complete tasks, such as planning research, preliminary or final designs, getting client approvals to key project milestones and so on. It was not long before his efforts came up against our indignation that we were being forced to cut corners and that the blame for delays was with third parties, not the in-house team. The head-to-heads on this got progressively more heated as we started feeling that our professional judgements were being questioned.

One member of our team had ingested the seventies bolshiness gene more than the rest of us, and he it was, who plotted the autocrat's downfall, and inevitably, soon afterwards, his own. The project in question progressed to the point where we needed to take our work to a key milestone presentation with the client - in Abu Dhabi, I recall, the focus by the early 1980s of huge new urban developments in which we played a significant part. The internal tensions of a team being harried to finish their research and preliminary designs quickly, had gone on for weeks, but the autocrat still chose to attend the client meeting with us. Not a wise move for him.

After the standard red-eyed overnight flight to the Gulf and faced with the usual client line-up of pristine white dishdashas and immaculate thobes across the acres of conference table, we duly ran through our master planning presentations covering site analyses, take up of industrial space, likely population build up and so on. But every question posed by the client was referred by our bolshie colleague to the autocrat for an answer. At first, by implication, but progressively via overt deferral to the autocrat as the higher authority present, the clear inference to be drawn was that we had been granted no time to do our work properly and that the autocrat's wiser counsel was needed. Of course, he had no more answers than did we; after all, he was a cost controller not an urban planner or engineer, and the meeting broke up to general expressions of inadequate progress. Sent home with a clear message to raise our game, the post-mortem back at base included what might be termed mutual vituperation. Neither party – neither the autocrat nor our bolshie colleague - survived for long but the time component in cost cutting soon relaxed somewhat with the departure of its unwelcome challenger. Professional judgement and quality outcomes eventually won out over timesaving for its own sake.

When relations in an office environment deteriorate further, the atmosphere becomes toxic. This poison is usually expressed as paranoia - who is saying what to whom and how does this threaten the previous carefully crafted status quo by which we all function? But paranoia is the symptom not the cause of toxicity - incompetence was invariably the root. I am lucky enough to have observed this kind of meltdown only rarely, and then only for short periods of time before measures were taken to correct it. But for some, they became the essence of office life and I had the peculiar sensation that some who seemed to be suffering most were also enjoying the circumstances most profoundly.

The autocrat had displayed incompetence as well as poor judgement and he paid the price. Such failures do not take long to be uncovered.

Dodging the psychopaths

I look back with broadly fond memories of office relations. Most people were quick to spot the best way for them to fit into the team, never the same for more than one at a time, because we all had different strengths and weaknesses on offer. As in all walks of life, there were always the occasional psychos whose social dysfunctionality appeared in many forms. Some were status conscious to a fault, wearing their role as team deputy leader or whatever, like a badge of honour, while others were the opposite, silent anarchists who thought team bonding a display of primitive behaviour to which they would not stoop. More common than any overtly anti-social behaviour, were those who seemed to suck oxygen out of the surrounding atmosphere. Negative behaviour to match this pattern took multiple forms including egocentrics, refusing to join in and contribute to team dynamics, and a few who delighted in ripping apart the reputations of others out of their earshot.

But you had to find ways to get on with everyone, because the belief that they were not contributing anything positive was probably mutual and they might have had hidden talents yet to be revealed. I recall one pompous so-and-so who was convinced that he was the techie wizard to solve all problems that we mere Neanderthals could only wonder at. Again, in the Middle East, this time in Yanbu, Saudi Arabia, we were lined up to do a major master plan presentation in front of a very prestigious audience of big shot sheiks. The techie wizard took charge of the new-fangled slide-changing gizmo activating the state-of-the art back projection kit, insisting that he would call the shots on the pace and style of the presentation.

After the standard delay of one hour to allow the dignitaries to arrive late (biggest shot always last), the presentation got under way. But the slide remote control device failed to respond to our techie wizard's efforts and the most powerful Sheik, who must have fancied himself as a techie super wizard, told him to push this button not that one or some such meaningless advice. Our techie did as he was bid … and the whole device promptly fell apart in his hands scattering across the floor. There was a sepulchral silence and I imagined two enormous eunuchs would step through the door and cart him off to a dungeon somewhere. The mighty Sheik waited a few seconds and stated quietly, "I told you to push it, not destroy it!" at which point, everyone fell about with real or forced laughter to break the ice.

After that, with our techie relieved of further slide changing duties, the presentation went well. The ice had been broken and the techie had finally found his role in our team – court jester to royalty - that he was wise enough to play along with in absence of any other outstanding talent.

Open plan in more ways than one
There was a kind of transition period between the pre digital, functional, sexually charged and hierarchical old days and the solely self-help, gender-blind and banter-free offices we inhabit now. We call it open plan and perhaps that does not just refer to the space. By the time I was becoming a department head or director of more than one project team, separate offices for the bosses were disappearing fast. I recall several of these were glass affairs through the nineties and noughties, because that seemed to strike the right balance between privacy to conduct personal performance reviews including tearing someone off a strip, while maintaining a freshly promoted transparency of governance. I remember the carefully contrived internal layouts with large indoor plants achieving a modicum of discreet privacy, their expense justified through the generation of a relaxed environment in which to conduct meetings. The glass-box privilege was provided on condition of sharing it with a conference table, such that, following a great display of democratic equanimity, I would vacate my space for meetings that I did not need to attend. I would sit in an empty space in the open office thinking myself, like other directors, the very model of the newly inclusive boss.

Alongside the shrinking of available space, gender balance has been the other big change, as many more women started entering our built environment professions. This has been almost wholly positive because it has upped the standards of professionalism no end, women showing themselves the match for, or better than, their male colleagues, and the males responding by sharpening their games. Engineering, whether civil, structural, mechanical, or electrical, still struggles to attract enough females to correct the imbalance. But planning with its strong, environmental (and thus apparently), caring image and to a lesser extent, architecture (still demanding massive testosterone-fuelled egos), are rightly succumbing to a more representative gender mix that reflects the graduate population at large.

Political correctness and the departments of Human Remains

Some functions disappeared altogether in the 1990s and beyond, including PA's to other than a whole department, as well as post rooms, travel sections and typists. Human Resources (or should that be 'Human Remains' in certain companies?) grew exponentially, replacing these diminishing administrative functions complementary to our professional activity. In my experience, this has not always been a positive move, inviting as it does, the belief that team relationships are a separate part of the working mechanism to the delivery of the professional outputs of our work. They are not. The boss – sometimes now termed the line manager - should always head up any HR responsibility because everyone including the boss, should be required to contribute to team dynamics and not treat them as a separate function. Beyond the bewildering world of employment law, HR should be the prime responsibility of the project and department team leader, not a professional trained solely to manipulate people's careers.

How have these shifts changed the atmosphere? There is still humour, but it treads lightly through sexual innuendo so much a rich source of badinage in the 1970s. The social, cultural and racial mix within teams has become so much more diverse and rightly so, but with this heterogeneity has been lost the self-assuredness that humour would be understood by most, if not all – let alone whether it was actually funny. We have not yet regained the confidence to take ourselves with a pinch of salt that used to leaven the daily round in a more homogeneous age. When that happens, we may have moved on from much of the social unease and political correctness that characterises the public working spaces we inhabit today.

I record these evolutions focusing on their socio-anthropological standpoints and in the near certainty that they will be recognisable across all professions and administrative functions for which office life is required. The 1970s were a knockabout decade socially, where people neither knew nor cared much for political correctness. True, there was much silent suffering as we now know at the hands of bullies, racists, sexual predators and the like, and I do not make light of the suffering that many endured. But still, the great majority of people of all races and both genders (there were only two in the 1970s) learned to handle the potentially aggressive social environment by skipping nimbly over its worst excesses of exploitation. I recall a pre-disposition to being bolshie when confronted was more common back then, otherwise standing up for oneself and not taking any shit. #MeToo? #MeNeither more like.

People quickly learned in former decades to adapt to the atmosphere of a place, whether it was empathetic or not with its different characters, kindnesses and cruelties. People usually found their feet as well as they could, no more nor lesser victims then than now, despite the more red-blooded atmosphere. I am not sure we are quite so adroit at feet-finding these days, because so much of the social exchange within offices is now curated carefully through health and safety, formulaic performance and salary reviews and the often-dead hand of an HR department that presumes to dictate how line managers should relate to their team.

Mental health is now rightly deemed a critical factor in the general welfare of any workforce, and much more is understood about it than five decades ago. It is entirely right that bullying or exploitative behaviour is called out, but I do not detect that mental well-being has significantly improved in the modern caring environment. Why might this be?

Sadly, it is because there remains far too much tokenism in properly managing mental health, combined with a tick-box mindset that substitutes checklists for real concern for how people fit in and fit together. This is hardly surprising because most office managers including those in human resources, are not trained in social psychology or behaviour dynamics; why should they be? Surely the welfare of any team is the responsibility of everyone in it including, of course, each individual. If you are unhappy, then there is ample opportunity to speak out that admittedly, relies on the sufferer having the confidence to do so. The most effective response to that is to listen, learn and act with discretion to the circumstances thereby revealed. That in turn, engenders the right culture in any office environment to encourage transparency, once again a function of good leadership rather than introduction of new procedures or professional skills only indirectly related to the business in hand.

Self-help the only option

Most offices of my acquaintance now offer virtually no support functions directly related to the necessary outputs of our work. Report production is admittedly structured through pre-defined templates, but the assembly of the text, the insertion of graphics, photos and the rest are expected to be entirely the responsibility of the author, using proprietary software but very much on his or her own. Travel arrangements to far flung continents albeit less obscure than hitherto as the world has opened up, have to jump through budget controlling and endless health, safety and security hoops, but again the traveller is alone in fixing her schedule and details.

I recall only a few years ago being faced with organising an urgent site visit with a client to a new town project in Sarawak, part of East Malaysia on the island of Borneo. A ground transport site visit across a region with few roads was simply impractical given the usual time pressures, so, after a fourteen-hour flight via Kuala Lumpur from London, a helicopter was going to be chartered to cover the ground. Helicopters? Of indeterminable safety standards? Flown by an unverifiable pilot crossing jungle and mountainous terrain? This crossed every red line of liability (the company's legal liability to me you understand, not my actual safety), until I agreed to make the trip in my own leave time, and thus outside of the standard corporate third-party cover. I survived to tell the tale and helped assemble a good bid for the master planning work that subsequently failed on price grounds. But of such backsliding nonsense as making the visit in my own time and thus, off the company register, is what so much of Health and Safety procedure is now comprised, when commercial interests butt up against so called managed risk envelopes. What a steaming pile of 'pony'!

There are now a whole range of due diligence vital actions needed of everyone from corporate professional development logs, via regular health and safety audits, to cross checks on appropriate use of the latest software applications. About the only relationship that resonates socially from the 1970s as between built environment professionals and the technical kit they need to do their jobs, is with the IT department. Here reside the high priests of techno with special brands of banter for those who spar with them to gain access to their techie wizardry. Tolerating the questionable hygiene standards of open biscuit packets and crushed coke cans littering their techno lair (known to us as the Radio Shack in the seventies), this banter ranges from sympathetic paternalism, at best, to sarcastically patronising, at worst. Those of us so technically illiterate as to be totally reliant on them suffer most. Perhaps I exaggerate, but IT geeks seem to need a lot of conversational massage to get from them what you really need, hardware fixes and software updates not only handed down but often custom-installed if your cards are played right. Empathy expended in droves – in both directions if you get the banter right.

Refreshments in the office environment are too often nowadays the time-pressed takeaway variety brought in for crumb-scattering across germ ridden and occasionally mouldy keyboards. Company dining rooms are long gone. The coffee or break-out area is often a soulless space despite some lurid décor, sometimes with tables for scoffing home-made or shop bought snacks but hardly inviting the sort of leisured conversation of old, where experiences shared might even cast light on the most complex commissioned briefs and tasks. The metaphor here for what has changed is the ubiquitous use of plastic knives and forks replacing the metal ones of the 1970s.

I recall vividly more leisured lunches of forty-five minutes or more during the seventies and eighties, in the staff canteens of the day, while grappling with a technical problem with no apparent solution. Sharing a table with a fellow or better yet, complementary professional and providing a five-minute summary of the problem either led to the bones of a solution or introduction to someone who knew someone. Too much of this excellent, if serendipitous network, is now replaced by the Internet where resides all you need, provided you ask the right question. There is a material difference between an online enquiry that might miss a few keywords and presenting a problem to a colleague who understands intuitively what is needed despite an inadequate definition. I had a wise old uncle when I was small whose metaphor for this situation was to hold an object one way, then to turn it around on its access. To a young mind, his suggestion that, "You should hold it horizontally," illustrated the point perfectly. Everything looks different from another angle.

Space dynamics

Offices have been limiting the available space to something less than the full employment complement for several years now, as people equipped with modern technology were being expected to work at home. Many preferred this, feeling more productive in their own domestic environment. In the last half year, these trends have exploded into a worldwide trend with the close down of offices to combat CV19 disease spreading. I cannot see a reversion to full office provision for all staff and expect instead, to see a requirement for individuals to book space in advance, if they want to come in. The ubiquitous influence of the office seems now to be waning and it will change the dynamics of team working profoundly.

If I were now running projects and their necessary multi-discipline teams, I would stress excessively that the team were not getting enough face time with me or their fellow team members. This has and always will, represent the glue, binding a successful project team and its eventual output and outcomes. I would insist, as I know many do, on days when the whole team appears in the office together once a week, or at least, if overseas, via video link, webinar or Zoom call. How else to maintain a sense of collective endeavour and ultimately, a common goal? If all this sounds old fashioned, then I will wear my dinosaur status with pride, but I cannot imagine how projects in my profession, calling on the vast range of specialist and common or garden skills can otherwise work to a client's eventual satisfaction. I cannot believe that any other service task dependant on team working could be any different.

Leadership: the ultimate face-to-face learning process

If there is one process in the office environment that can never work online, it is creating the future generations of team leaders. So much of what we learn from our peers and seniors is non-verbal and dependent on face-to-face experience. Tone would be the single description for how to identify either good leadership or bad. Observing a boss dealing with situations either technical, contractual, or purely human, is critical for the next generation to discover how to get on in each social environment. This cannot be done online. Body language, tone and timbre of voice, eye contact, knowing when to intervene or not do so at all and many, many more, are the actions and behaviour characteristics that are observed minutely by the emotionally intelligent, and they cannot be substituted on screen.

Like my fear of lost face-to-face contact with a project team resulting from too much working remotely, I fear for the future advancement of those selected to take charge of technical teams or business processes in the future. Their means of recognition of how it is done best or worst – the latter often proving as instructive as the former – is only properly gained in person. The wise bosses of business and professional services will ensure that as soon as possible, they revert to a manageable minimum of full presence of their teams together physically in offices. Working together needs to mean just that for effective team bonding.

Individualism lives

Having experienced the old hierarchical style of office environment and witnessed its gradual evolution to modern layouts and protocols, I have also observed some extraordinary reactions to the homogenisation of space and procedure. For example, those evolutions that amounted to a loss of status expressed through a range of factors such as space, privacy, admin or secretarial support and the like have been the main battlegrounds. But they are all instructive of a common theme: individuality faced with, and kicking back, against conformity. People have become a lot more conventional and almost a-political in the modern era, but individual resistance to mindless authority is still prevalent and all the more noticeable for that. It is the sandpaper that not only scratches and irritates the smooth operational surface but ensures that surface remains shiny and clear. Shiny clarity in this context is good.

I recall vividly the amazing, if ultimately, insignificant case of The Personal Coffee Mugs. For a long time after offices had become open plan, the breakout kitchen area was pretty much the only place where people could meet and chat. It might have been possible at your desk, but with others working diligently close at hand and thus eavesdropping on a conversation when it might be getting interesting, it usually meant that the working space was kept for quick fire repartee and little more. More meaningful conversation needed segregation to the break-out kitchen area - or of course, the pub down the road.

In the kitchens, people could store their snacks and personalised coffee mugs. This started with some scope for individuality in tastes and personal crockery. After our boutique consultancy of some two hundred people had been bought out (merged was the official term, but there is never such a thing as merger, they always end up as takeovers), we moved to a larger office to join our new colleagues and a larger break out area equipped with dishwasher, boiling water faucet (that everyone had to be taught how to use under health and safety rulings) and a series of standard issue new company logoed mugs for tea and coffee. Oh joy. Some of those whose integration into the new operation was proving less perfect than that defined in the HR textbook, brought their own mugs with them. Most of these had been in use over years, some with their own humpty dumpty legs and feet to stand on, others with dubious messages and almost all, with years of coffee or tea stain residue. Cleanliness was not a priority with this personal crockery, but it was much loved.

The maintenance staff, who cleaned the kitchens, complained to the new authorities that the personal mugs were not being put in the dishwasher and cluttered up the draining boards after very casual rinsing which was as much hygiene as any of them had experienced over years. Listeria lurked and personal coffee mugs were subsequently banned, but only to disappear into office desk drawers to be brought out for loving use and furtively put away afterwards. Washing up became even rarer for the diehard owners of the now officially discouraged personal crockery. Listeria continued to lurk.

It was only a matter of time before personal desk space was also under review, as the policy of only providing about seventy-five per cent of the capacity theoretically required by the employee headcount started to impact. HR and maintenance did not expect everyone to be in simultaneously though of course, project and line managers often wanted to do things differently (quite right too). So, with hot desking in operation, there was, in theory, nowhere for personal coffee mugs to be hidden. But the desk space regulars who effectively retained their own space, became resistance-style collaborators in the subterfuge, enabling themselves and more irregular visitors to use personal crockery other than company-logo embellished vessels. Individualism was briefly triumphing.

The forces of conformity were now affronted and in one overnight act of shocking privacy invasion, HR endorsed maintenance to go through desk drawers and extract said personal crockery and impound it. After all, by now, the desks had now been re-classified as public not private space. Notices were posted inviting claimants to take back their crockery, but few wanted to do so. The mugs had become a symbol of independence rather than an artefact of intrinsic value. Eventually, the unclaimed mugs were disposed of and the sad sight of them discarded in a clear recycling bag was photographed leaving the building one lunchtime - but forever. There is no glorious dénouement or punch line to this story with victory won by the personal coffee mug brigade. A little individuality just died that day.

Mental health as the canary in the mine

There has been a huge increase in the awareness of mental health across not only offices but urban environments in general. *The Thought Report, Health, Poverty Action, Psychology Today* and the recently much maligned World Health Organisation provide excellent sources or direct references where to find what constitutes the healthy office. The best of these identify culture as the core of the most positive working environments. But too many restrict themselves to physical environments such as the comfort of good seating and posture, light, breakout areas and space allocation between individual workstations.

I have worked – often temporarily overseas by good fortune - in some shockingly bad physical environments. Broken air conditioning and furniture, lack of fresh air and adequate lighting are bad enough, but they pale beside bad leadership of the team. You can forgive an awful lot of the physical inadequacy if the attitude of leadership is right. I recall one frozen winter day in a new office in the UK, where the central heating failed. The boss called everyone together, apologised and admitted there had been a cockup and people were free to go home if they preferred. Of course, he knew full well he had no choice under law, but in an office of over one hundred staff, not one left the building after that. They just wanted acknowledgement that things needed to be put right. When we eventually got compensation back from the landlord (it took eighteen months), the money was put in a staff fund to buy sports equipment for the social club. That was a happy office.

Why have I chosen offices as a metaphor for the gradual decline observable in otherwise free-wheeling human relations? It is because offices remain one of the most common marketplaces for interaction between the personal and the public domain. Nowhere else do we find such rules of engagement for the way people get on with each other in public space, sometimes invisible, but more and more often these days via written guidelines. This may well be due for radical change as we emerge from lockdowns despite which business and commerce have continued remotely. Will we need such huge office floorspace in the future? Time will tell, but while town centres may change radically, the loss of human interaction that offices provide may be a more profound change to society. This will do nothing for building connections between people and teams.

We have already observed during the early months of learning to live with CV19 that there have been significant increases in mental disturbance of people in both domestic and work-related circumstances. It is too early to be citing statistical data, but we know, for example, that women's refuges against abusive partners have been overwhelmed with requests for shelter. Living and working purely in the domestic environment may be a short-term solution to the need for social distance, but it is not a solution to the problems of mental health. The office is the marketplace for teams that work together as well occasionally apart, and their continued use to check on not only work and project progress but personal welfare is essential. To that extent, the role of the office in bringing people together will continue to be critical to mental wellbeing.

Reduced dependence on offices may be a permanent feature of change after the pandemic but they cannot be replaced altogether. Offices are cockpits of human interaction and their evolving use may be a perfect metaphor for the social evolutions I have witnessed throughout my career. So much of what you once learned of behaviour in the office is now written down. The more this interaction is curated by rules and regulations, introduced because of the diversity of cultures, languages and values, so much less marked in my early career, the less we learn how to cope with such diversity for ourselves. With heightened sensitivity about political, racial, cultural, sexual or gender awareness, not to mention safety and security of employees, it is understandable that our public lives are surrounded by regulation. But with each new advisory guideline – acceptable behaviour in all but name - a little more of our capacity to judge for ourselves and thus develop self-reliance is lost. This too is a loss for empathy and building meaningful relations, because these only really work when people are allowed to think for themselves.

The recent arrival of CV19 and subsequent lockdown of office space, as part of a universal battle to reduce its spread, will have long term implications for offices. Already, far more business has proved sustainable using online media than managers and bosses thought was possible. The ubiquitous email, social media such as LinkedIn (Facebook with ties on) online meetings and webinars, already well-established within parts of most business environments, have assumed centre stage while face-to-face meetings and simply working together in the same place are impossible. Will we revert to anything resembling even the mildly dystopian atmosphere that I had already alluded to pre-CV19? Or will the prevailing wisdom, dictated by the cost controllers, determine that offices are a thing of the past and everyone can carry on working in their little home-based cells?

As you might imagine, I earnestly hope for a return to physical team proximity. No team bonding or harmonious working arrangements can thrive while people cannot get to know each other. And you cannot really get to know each other relying solely on on-line communications, where body language, facial expression and simply hanging out together remain the principal ingredients of any move from mere acquaintance to team bonding and friendship.

However, all is not negative as a result of our self-isolation. The heart-warming expressions of community spirit, and neighbours reaching out to each other, when previously, they might have passed each other in the street, suggests that there remains a profound sense that we all need each other and that there is at least as much of a glow of satisfaction from helping, as being helped – probably more. It just means that in the pandemic world we now inhabit, the tension between so called efficient working methods and effective team bonding will be greater than ever. I know which side of the battle lines I will be on. There is no substitute for understanding people when wanting to work well together and there is no alternative to doing so face-to-face when seeking to achieve this. For me, the office remains the main crucible of bonding with our fellow workers and we cannot rely only on remote working to replace it.

Chapter 5

Coping with Trauma

Trauma is nothing new and it ruins lives for invisibly large numbers of people even widening fractures in relationships between nations. This chapter focuses on regions of the world that seem recently to have suffered more than most. Neighbouring population displacements are affecting other areas such as Europe and North America because we live in a small and now highly interconnected world.

*

Experiencing major traumas can ruin lives. But is it still possible that trauma victims can exhibit greater empathy for others because of the pain and suffering they themselves have experienced? Trauma at both personal and collective scale is clearly a source of fracture within communities and between nations. With a focus on Middle East society and cultures, I am going to look at trauma impacts on community morale together with how people there perceive themselves and visitors passing through. By examining the impacts of various types of trauma on people, I aim to find out if they are help or hindrance in the quest for greater human understanding.

My approach is deliberately pitched at the experience-based and anecdotal end of the analytical spectrum, more of a street-wisdom approach to examining the situation. This is based on my work and travels through the region over several decades during which I encountered diverse examples of trauma both before and after periods of violence or civil upheaval. For those seeking more extensive academic references, there are plenty of these to be found through, for example the UK's *Journal of Clinical Psychiatry*, and publications of the Royal College of Psychiatry, or in North America, the American Psychiatric Association and Academy of Experts in Traumatic Stress.

In fact, I will start with one academic reference which I think is particularly interesting because of the way it has subsequently been applied within the community. This was the Cardiff Traumatic Stress Initiative led by Professor Jonathan Bisson at the city's university of which I am proud to be a postgraduate (though in a wholly separate subject). Written up in the Royal College of Psychiatry Bulletin in 2003, its worldwide impact on management of trauma may have been due to its extended implementation of treatments into the community, addressing among other conditions, Post-Traumatic Stress Disorder (PTSD).

My approach is bound to be much more unrepresentative of the wider issues that assail individuals and society in general, but hopefully, will still be valuable. With this limitation, there is still a wide horizon of geographies and situations from which I have drawn personal conclusions. Given the circumstances of recent pandemic, with its multiple effects on social wellbeing and confidence in the future, this might prove useful, the combination of a philosophical and experience-based approach in counterpoint to psychological, psychiatric and therefore, academic ones available elsewhere.

I conclude with a review of how Maslow's hierarchy of human needs as instructive, determining the extent to which individuals can deal successfully with trauma as a function of where on Maslow's needs hierarchy an individual resides.

Experience of war and PTSD

I am hugely fortunate, like most of my generation in western Europe to have no experience of war. But I am the first of many generations through my father's line, to have been able to say that. We have become complacent about that, assuming war to be aberrant, but in many of the places I have visited throughout the world, it is a reality, happening now or acting as a deep impact on recent memories.

The psychological impacts of war – in its worst form, PTSD – are now well documented though unique to individual cases. I am sure my father will have suffered from it, if only in a mild form after six years of war between 1939 and 1945, well before I was born. Like most soldiers, the periods of intense risk of injury or death will have been short – in his case the beaches of Dunkirk, tank and artillery engagements through North Africa and Italy but possibly most profoundly, the seven month grinding battles of attrition through the atrocious winter weather at Monte Cassino between Naples and Rome in 1943-44.

Like any young boy looking up to his dad with pride, I was fascinated by his experiences. But I never remember him talking to me about the violence, death and injury he must have witnessed regularly. He would focus on the apparently ridiculous aspects of military life – the mismatch of equipment with need whether food, shelter or occasionally weapons, the stupidity or vainglory of rank-conscious individuals (rarely correlated with their seniority), and the humour, always the humour - of being the only Welsh officer in a lowland Scottish regiment. This was dealt with by saying he only really felt safe when they were fighting the Germans, otherwise the Glaswegians would be fighting each other. But I suspect this humour was only another way of dealing with combat stress and I don't mean to diminish the horrors of war in their multiple forms with this account (and also, I love Glasgow).

I am sure my dad was lucky enough, though he did stop a bullet in a lethal ambush in thickly wooded terrain north of Perugia in June 1944. Of that incident, I mainly recall him laughing because they had arrested a German relieving himself behind a farmhouse only for his pals to shoot and kill two of the arresting party and wounding my dad. He told me it did not hurt to start with, and he was able to escape. He just remembered the newly liberated German running down the field bare-arsed, with his trousers round his ankles.

This is not heroism unless you accept that making light of pain, suffering and fear is a kind of heroism. Some now regard that as unhelpful and that you must express your anxiety as openly as possible in order to overcome it. PTSD was sparsely, if ever dealt with, even after the horrors of the First World War, despite academic and clinical psychology being rapidly growing fields of medicine. By the end of the Second World War, it was well enough understood, but the capacity to deal with it was scarcely defined and almost wholly under-provided in the face of what was probably huge unspoken demand. Most people just got on with life to recover slowly with the healing of time. Some will not have done and that is an injustice.

Trauma at the private scale

With deliberate contrast to my father's war experience, I offer a very different personal trauma from my early teenage years, a metaphor for the contrast between my father's generation and my own. Theirs were so often public traumas familiar to many in multiple forms, while mine was much more individual and privately endured.

Between the ages of eleven and fourteen, with hormones raging through my anatomy, I periodically suffered the debilitating condition of boils. Usually (mercifully), they appeared one at a time, but sometimes two or more would slowly gather on the back of my neck or backside and ensure a degree of discomfort that lasted several days. Sitting awkwardly was just about possible, but occasionally, they would appear on the side of my torso and these were the most painful of all, as the flesh is thin there and my arm would brush the tender area around the gathering, only making things worse.

There are far more painful conditions that other children suffer, of which mental disorders are the least visible yet most profound. But this was my own, if irregular, private hell. The debilitating restriction on free movement including sports at school made me feel excluded. Part of this was that the condition did not bear being spoken about. In my own mind, there was something unclean about the malign gatherings of pus that set me aside from others. I suffered in silence at school until they burst painfully or subsided. Little did I know how common they were with others, because so many of us suffered in silence and seemingly therefore, alone. Thinking back, it was the non-physical aspect of self-doubt that was the worst aspect and I wrongly considered the condition to be mine alone.

At home, there was some parental sympathy. My mum sought to offer a compensatory homily that those who suffer become more sympathetic to the suffering of others, regardless of the condition. I think she may have been talking about empathy though that word was not much used at the time. Usually, my dad displayed his sympathy through humour, thinking it best to distract me. Knowing he had been through far worse, I laughed along with his sometimes-feeble jokes and just got on with it.

Though a pretty minor teenage complaint that disappeared in time, it was still trauma of sorts that I recall occasionally. I think back now to my mother's claim that it would make me more sympathetic. She may have been right – parents often are – because the thought of no longer suffering, occasionally made me look at others who might be continuing to do so, for whatever reason, with a touch more compassion. I had sometimes been drawn while at prep school, to some people's otherness, and this continued as my own private sebaceous hell subsided as I grew older.

As just one other example, (less common then than now), fat people were often the butt of minor cruelties and sometimes worse. But I sensed some of their pain while sometimes shamefully repelled by their physical appearance. Getting people to talk about their feelings concerning others' perceptions seemed a minor triumph, as I felt it was a form of meaningful connection that was mostly left unexplored. There is a common perception that in boarding schools, this sort of confessional is rare if not non-existent. I disagree. We seemed to have time to get to understand each other better in circumstances of mundane domestic as well as academic and social exposure. I do not remember the confidences shared as a result ever being breached to others. Trust is a critical factor in getting at true feelings.

One thing for sure, those – and there were many - who seemed to have no such feelings were glaringly obvious to me as thick-skinned beings, hewn from coarser clay. They probably rejoiced in their superior capacity to cope with life's challenges – if they thought about that sort of thing at all. I held such types in quiet contempt, though in my older age, I suspect they were fewer in number than I thought at the time. I now think the great majority of people are sensitive to seeking connection with others in some unique form if they can only overcome shyness or anal retention to be able to reach out. We are all members of a common herd as well as individuals after all.

Traumas at a national scale
Clearly at an individual level dealing with trauma will differ with every case and the context in which one experiences suffering or feels the need to connect – reaching out, as Americans say. But how does this need for connections play out

in the wider social realm? Do societies that experience a disproportionate level of suffering also exhibit empathy in greater measure than others? I have visited several countries that have experienced more than their fair share of suffering – Vietnam and Colombia to name two, as we shall see later. But the Middle East probably retains the greatest recent sources of widespread suffering of any of the world's regions. I have visited many of its countries mainly for work and less so for tourism, namely from west to east, Morocco, Algeria, Tunisia, Libya, Egypt, Lebanon, Turkey, Iran, Kuwait, Saudi Arabia, Bahrain, Qatar, UAE and Oman. Plenty of sad history to provide context for suffering among that list.

Regardless of whether countries are now popular tourist destinations, such as Morocco, Egypt, UAE or Oman, my itineraries presented many opportunities to encounter turmoil and civil unrest, together with the personal and social trauma that accompanies it. Sadly, a disproportion of the world's troubles of the last seventy years and more, emanate from the Middle East. That seems likely to continue.

As neither soldier nor journalist, I have usually managed to avoid places and periods of open conflict. But I have witnessed many of the growing tensions building before, as well the long drawn out pain after, better-publicised periods of violence across several of the region's theatres of war. For any student of empathy and its polar opposite, these build ups and aftermaths are as important as the headline grabbing outbursts of violence themselves – perhaps more so. There is so little time for meaningful connections with people while experiencing the immediate shock of violent hostilities and open warfare. Survival is then the all-consuming priority.

But in the still times before and after conflict, there is a different – perhaps more reflective – period. This is trauma associated either with the dread of what may be coming, or afterwards when a kind of peace may be re-established, but when the pain and suffering for lost loved ones, and the disorder to civil society, become long and bitter legacies acknowledged only in mourning by individual hearts and minds. So, it is worth looking either side of the wars to study the roots and leftovers from the trouble. They are profound.

The Middle East as a crucible for suffering

Suffering the consequences of traumatic events is bad enough, but reactions to the underlying reasons for the troubles from which they emerge are just as deep. The passions aroused by such politics are often in direct proportion to the sense of inability to influence events for the better. Democracy grants a small measure of relief from powerlessness, but there is precious little democracy in most Middle East societies.

Conflicts between contrasting cultural aspirations are a common theme running through most upheavals in the Middle East, often more prevalent than elsewhere. These bear brief examination to understand the context of much that is deep-rooted in the region's societies. These differing aspirations take many forms, but in very broad terms, a traditional view of society's destiny seen from a conservative Muslim perspective within the embrace of an all-seeing deity, is pitted against an aggressive modernism and adherence to non-spiritual and materialistic values. In many western societies, we have accommodated ourselves to separating the material from the spiritual, but in many Muslim cultures this is regarded as a sell-out of true faith – a denial of the fundamental of God or Allah being behind and ahead of all physical progress, sustaining it from beneath and seeing it in context from above.

As I will explain in a more biographical chapter to follow, I have been a participant in many urban master planning projects throughout the Middle East. So, I have probably been responsible for importing some of the materialist - a.k.a. western – values, as seen from a fundamentalist or traditionalist viewpoint. I might have been a bearer of modernism or a crusader, to quote one of my life-long Arab friends. I think he is being either humorous or ironic, as we worked a lot together on development projects and he shares much of my outlook and professional experience, albeit from a respectful stance in relation to Muslim traditions. There may be a more serious undertone to his description; it is certain that the term crusader has a very different flavour within the chosen vocabulary of fundamentalists.

Both modernist and traditional philosophies in Arab and Persian societies are either underpinned, or perhaps overlain, by a deep sense of lost civilisation and cultural sophistication for which the region was renowned throughout our own European middle ages. When we in the west were still submerged by monarchic autocracies and feudalism, Arab and Persian societies were not only militarily powerful and centres of relatively enlightened government, but leaders in astronomy, mathematics, medicine, cartography and navigation, both marine and terrestrial, architecture, town planning and the finest (abstract) art. Left to its multiple selves, the region may well have flourished for a long time as one or more centres of world civilisation. This was not to be.

First, rulers in western Europe including England, France, Spain, Italian city states including the once powerful Venice, the Vatican and the Holy Roman Empire comprising much of Germany and Austria, intent on diverting attention from their own internal troubles, invoked Christianity in a confected casus belli to re-capture the Holy Land. The Crusades of the twelfth and thirteenth centuries and their aftermath, set the tone for a toxic relationship between Jewish, Muslim and Christian beliefs that has survived to the present day. Subsequently, as the west gained material advantage through imperialist commerce, then industrial revolution and its multiple technologies, the Middle East fell into relative decline in relation to Europe's progressively more outward looking but materialist trading economies. Later still, at the end of the First World War, our colonialist disposition saw to the carving up of Arab, Ottoman and Persian lands, forcing them, through leaderships allied to the west, into states of competitive disadvantage and to adopt similar material values to our own.

The extent to which Christianity and Judaism have accommodated themselves more easily to social materialism than the Muslim faith is the subject of a book in its own right, but sufficient here to say that mutual religious misunderstanding frequently leading to intolerance and worse, has characterised our relations for hundreds of years. It shows little sign of diminishing. The majority of states in the region now ruled by autocratic governments, struggle for supremacy over narrowly defined theocracies or, on rare occasions, the uncoordinated forces of liberalisation and democracy. Many of the problems of the area are now entirely home grown, but the hand of the west is usually there under the surface, as a conscious or unconscious catalyst to civil tension and struggle.

My timing of visits to countries such as Algeria, Iran and Kuwait brought me close to the edges of violence, either on the verge of breaking out or having just happened. These precursors and aftermaths of violent times and their associated trauma, namely fear, or actual bereavement for lost loved ones or the loss of homes, homelands and tranquillity, were all too self-evident. You could sense it when things were soon to explode, and you could feel the drawn-out pain and bitterness afterwards. Perhaps such traumas run deeper than the shocked reactions to the violence itself. Psychological impacts run deep, are long lasting and take unpredictable directions as the more learned observers of such conditions would be far more effective at explaining than me.

The domestic realm in Middle Eastern societies

In recent times, the horrors the region has suffered – in Libya, Syria and Yemen, for example – have produced major trauma for the populations of those countries and continue to do so. Across the region, the multi-faceted death struggle between autocratic governments, forces promoting democracy and open government and religious fundamentalists, drags on in too many locations. It is all too easily forgotten by those of us watching from relatively more tranquil places, that the great majority of the Middle Eastern people, want a peaceful life to raise their families and improve their lot, drawing the line at doing so at the expense of others. Despite their numbers and thus their unrealised potential to be the strongest voice in society, such middle of the road family values are squeezed between those who fight over different visions of each country's future and the high ground of news-making that it attracts. Violence always drowns out more peaceful aspiration, but it cannot last forever.

I am lucky enough to have known several families in the region from within this silent majority who yearn like the rest of us for a more tranquil environment. Through their peaceful welcome and fundamental decency based on the centuries' long tradition of hospitality, the chance to discuss the ills of their societies emerge slowly but steadily. They have been all the more precious for that.

There is little censorship apparent at the personal level. It is then that the real trauma can be glimpsed as individuals shyly admit to having friends, or even family, who had taken a different path to their own and been locked into one or other extremes of the violence that sits just beneath the surface of normal life. Worse still, there have been those who sought neither side in the endless conflicts but were just caught up in the crossfire both literal and metaphoric, blighting lives forever. Hearing their stories of suffering makes for hard listening.

I am convinced there is a silent majority of families who privately renounce both extremes of autocracy and fundamentalism but stop short of activism in favour of democratic government because they fear the ruthless suppression that would ensue. It is too easy for westerners to accuse this of being collaborationist – family safety and security comes first. Nor are they overt supporters of western style capitalist democracy of which I, and fellow project colleagues from the west, were assumed to be ambassadors. They know their history only too well and know that the west will suit itself first and the inhabitants second if it comes to regime change.

They simply want peace to bring up their children in the way they want. What I have often encountered and found to be humbling, is a determination to welcome foreigners of whatever point of view, precisely because they wish to dispel the hostile image that their region portrays to the outside world. It is almost as if they are saying, "Our system of government may be dysfunctional, our society no better, and we are all suffering multiple traumas of loss and bereavement. But to counteract that, we maintain the best of Arab (or Persian) traditions of hospitality at home. We are going to honour these through you as our guest! Let the public domain look after itself, but in private you are welcome. Ahlan wa sahlan! Khosh amadid! Welcome, welcome!" Truly, this amounts to awareness with the condition in which they find themselves and a desire to want visitors to understand. Making meaningful connections with understanding strangers seems doubly important as it renders their suffering and disillusion less lonely.

Family values of the region are mirrored to some extent in the design and layout of the traditional Middle Eastern home, a house surrounding an external courtyard that looks in on itself, thereby turning its back on the outside world with almost no external fenestration. It was and sometimes remains, a physical statement that the family looks after its own while wider society and governments, are not trusted to do so.

Traditionally, the female half of the population was thus given the means to guard a modest privacy from the gaze of and social interaction with third parties – in particular, non-family males. This segregation of half the population from the other half is alien to our western sociology and values. But once we are over being affronted by this, we would do well to reflect that it is only a century and a half, since similar social mores were widely prevalent in the west, albeit by then, starting to disappear.

For us in the west, these changes in gender dynamics coincided with progressive industrialisation and wartime economics, during which women steadily engaged within the workforce beyond domestic service or the near slavery of mining or agricultural labour. As industrialisation has only been replicated across the Middle East in a very recent and partial way, and crucially not engaging the whole of the indigenous population, it is little surprise that there has been only slow movement to a more emancipated relationship between the genders.

The major drag on more widespread integration of the sexes in the region has been religious conservatism. From my occasional and wholly unscholarly readings of the Koran, I have been unable to find any references to women as secondary to men. On the contrary, there are many of the one hundred and fourteen surahs in the holy book of Islam where men are exhorted to treat women as equals, albeit that they were permitted to take more than one wife, provided each was treated with equal respect. Even this social and religiously endorsed pattern has a substantial historical precedent. During the early wars between the emerging Islamic state and neighbouring Christians and Jews during the (Christian) years 600AD to 800AD, huge numerical losses of males of military age were suffered in battle, such that the only protection available for the many widowed wives and children was their absorption into other families. Surviving warriors adopted and thus protected the women and children involved.

This medieval form of social welfare – a means of dealing with PTSD if you like - was the wellspring for social patterns that survive today, but in practice nowadays, only for the wealthiest able to support more than one wife. Questions abound about how marital dynamics can be maintained equably in such circumstances, but the roots of this social trend were as much demographic as they were an expression of a religiously conservative lifestyle. I cannot find where it might also be part of Muslim theocracy.

In recent times, such family patterns have sometimes been corrupted into a power and control trope where for many women in the most conservative countries, the rights that we have come to expect in the west such as voting, holding bank accounts, running businesses, driving a car or even being allowed to travel unaccompanied, are only slowly being introduced, let alone accepted up and down the generations. But western and feminist indignation does not always help. Things will move at the pace of those directly involved; we can only hope that it will be the woman's voice that will progressively become the one that is heard.

Fundamentalism to terrorism

With all the social conflict that prevails in so many Middle Eastern societies, there should be little wonder that a small but significant minority have turned to fundamentalism in one form or another. The search for an identity is critical to dealing with the impacts of trauma and the desperation that is a precursor to individual espousal of violence, needs to be understood if it is to be dealt with effectively. I doubt I would even have known for sure if I had been in the presence of a fundamentalist fanatic, clothing him or herself in the self-righteousness of their interpretation of Islamic tradition. Of course, they would never have admitted it to me unless they had also decided that my time was up. Still here to tell the tale, I am guessing that we only ever passed like silent ships in the night.

But I do wonder sometimes how close might have been such encounters. Those espousing fundamentalist views are just as likely to be living near me in London as they might be well – or badly - met on the streets of Dubai or Riyadh. Many fundamentalists born and living in the west have very little concept of what life is really like in the modern Middle East. I cannot say, in our polarised world, whether I could now come to understand first-hand an Islamic fundamentalist worldview. It would be difficult enough to achieve the access to even hear it expounded first-hand. However, there surely remains a kernel of goodwill in almost everybody with which exploration of common ground, if not congruent opinions should be possible. That much would amount to the beginnings of meaningful connection, but few chances now exist to agree to disagree.

Algeria – An absence of macro, social scale empathy

For about a decade from the mid-seventies to the mid-eighties, I worked in and out of Algeria on a variety of urban and infrastructure projects across the country, from Annaba in the east, the capital Algiers itself, to the University town of Tlemcen in the west. During this decade, internal resistance was steadily growing to the inflexibly autocratic socialist and post-colonial government. I was struck by the dour and sometimes humourless nature of many Algerian clients, usually government staff of one Ministry or Municipality or another, charged with getting things built. They often resented the need to engage western professionals such as we planners, architects and engineers, because our branch of large-scale master planning was not much understood in the region at the time. For many, this resentment will have originated from a pre-disposition against westerners (northerners, in the case of Algeria) through the recently terminated colonial rule of France, then only a few years after a vicious eight-year war of independence.

The implacable resistance to previous French occupation may have contributed to the inability of the post-colonial Algerian government to treat their own people with openness and transparency. If true, like many children of violent parents, this will have been a clear example of those brutalised by the independence struggle, passing this on to those whom the freedom fighters had liberated. The absence of empathy at a macro, social scale during that decade was clear to me, evidence that previous violence and its associated trauma was no seedbed for better understanding and tolerance afterwards, quite the opposite.

In 1975, all of sixteen years before the outbreak of a ruinous civil war across the whole of Algeria between forces of socialist modernity and Islamic fundamentalism, I watched from the illusory safety of a hotel balcony in Annaba, early manifestations of this turmoil, namely a massive people's march protesting unemployment, poverty and the apparent indifference of the government to the peoples' suffering. It was brutally repressed, but largely away from the march and therefore, out of sight. I learned only later of the repression from some of those who had marched, reporting furtively to observers such as me who had gained their trust. They spoke of ringleaders being rounded up, incarcerated and tortured, long after the public demonstrations had dispersed. At the time, the discontent seemed to have been suppressed, but it was only simmering under the surface. Several subsequent demonstrations in Tlemcen, Oran and principally, the capital, Algiers, were met with similar quiet but ruthless repression by an obdurate socialist government.

The conflicting views of how Algeria was to evolve – via a socialist interpretation of modernism or a return to traditional, fundamentalist and theocratic values, went right to the heart of Arab and Berber dilemmas about their future. In late 1991, open violence finally erupted into a civil war, at least as vicious as the independence struggle against France of four decades previously. Indeed, it was worse, in that both sides were native Algerians with nowhere to go but to fight in their own streets and countryside for their conflicting visions of a future homeland. It also lasted longer than the struggle for independence, fully eleven agonising years until early 2002. The wounds are still there right across Algerian society both at home and among the diaspora of those who have left.

Iran – Silence is not always golden
In Iran in 1978, and only a few febrile months before the revolution against the Shah, I became sure I could smell fear in crowds. I also got caught up in a security check around which the threat of violence played through the imagination, perhaps as menacingly as the real thing.

During these last days of the Shah's regime, I was part of an academic delegation attending an urban planning conference in Teheran. That is how I found myself with others easily distinguishable as Europeans and Americans visiting the capital's Grand Bazaar. At the time, opposition to the Shah was acute but still under cover. The west was clearly seen to be on the side of the government, preserving the Pahlavi dynasty that it had put in place twenty-five years previously to protect British and US oil interests. The bazaars – or souks in Arab countries – have always been the focus of economic and therefore, social interaction in such communities and thus, the place where hostility to the status quo might be expected to emerge first. Teheran was no different, and a gathering of mainly white males taking an overt, if innocent interest in the centuries old layout and function of the marketplace, was bound to attract interest.

Given the timing, place and context, our interest started to attract unwelcome looks. It is difficult looking back over forty years to pinpoint the symptoms of this hostility, but I recall body language as conveying more about how we were being perceived than anything overt, either said or done. Shoppers turned their backs and merchants, usually keen to encourage would-be buyers with a gushing welcome, seemed reluctant to draw us to their stalls and wares. In a normally bustling atmosphere that I recall, which surprisingly, still included the unloading of camels in the caravanserai courtyards, it was the silence with which we were met that was most menacing. Clearly, the legendary reputation for hospitality was in temporary abeyance and we felt it wise to withdraw before more obvious displays of disapproval occurred.

In notable contrast, that evening, we were honoured guests of a high-end reception attended by senior government, military and royal dignitaries, assembled to celebrate the inauguration of a major new urban development on the edge of the capital, named Shahestan Pahlavi. Its name, only revealed for the first time to warm applause that evening, was indicative of the tendency of powerful rulers to build monuments after their own image. Truly an example of Shelley's Ozymandias, King of Kings!

There was a lot of swank on display; government ministers, senior military with medals and braid and their heavily bejewelled wives, and occasional but obviously minted property developers, wearing sleek suits tailored in Paris, Milan or Savile Row. Enthusiastic approval of this latest example of the Shah's benevolent munificence was the order of the day. Yet after the formalities of speeches and expressions of mutual international esteem, all the Iranian guests left promptly in security-escorted chauffeur driven convoys, as protection against threats of attack from hostile opposition groups beyond the confines of the hotel. Being out on the streets was not safe. We foreign visitors, left to ourselves in the near empty hotel ballroom, looked around us and drew a collective anticipatory breath of something about to happen of which we were not yet sure.

A few days later, during the return trip to London, Teheran airport was heaving with families of all kinds – rich, poor, urbanites and country people, and a high proportion of religious types in traditional clothing with their womenfolk fully veiled, all looking to get out of the capital or the country as a whole. In the endless queues, there seemed to be real fear among these travellers, that this last check by state security would detain them more permanently.

I knew how they felt, because the previous day a group of us had returned from Isfahan and had been questioned one by one in an intimidating manner by security police because of a mismatch between passport identities and airline tickets. You could smell fear as rank odour in the waiting queues to board the aircraft before and after passport control.

Scattered protests and strikes against the Pahlavi dynasty had commenced over eighteen months before, getting more openly defiant each time. By February 1979, the last royal ruler of Iran had fled, and an Islamic government had taken over. Royalty of another kind, defined by theocracy rather than monarchy, has ruled since. Sadly, I have not been back; it was and is, a beautiful country and has adopted its own way forward to development and progress with much reduced social or trading interface with the west. The misunderstanding between the two value systems is almost total and we are both the poorer for that, but I have some understanding of why and how it happened. Nationwide isolation and trauma are on full display.

Kuwait – Trauma for just about everyone

I have visited Kuwait many times, both before and after the First and Second Gulf Wars of the 1990s and early 2000s and have spoken with many local friends and project colleagues of their memories of the Iraqi occupation. This was a traumatic experience for Kuwaitis, as Sadam Hussein's army seized what he claimed to be rightfully Iraqi territory before the British had carved it off from the previous Mesopotamian province of the Ottoman Empire after 1919. Kuwaitis dispute this interpretation, strongly claiming that Kuwait had been independent for centuries and were offered protection by the British motivated early in the twentieth century by oil and gas reserves. But who writes the history books? Take your pick of the interpretations, but it is usually the victors.

Through the second half of 1990, resistance to the occupying Iraqis took many forms, including quiet and valiant support of foreign expatriates in hiding and holed up and undiscovered in their villas for weeks on end, while food and water was supplied to them clandestinely. Anything more overt by way of defiance to the occupying forces was usually met with brutal repression and Kuwaitis recounting their experiences afterwards still felt it deeply. I recall the subsequent accounts from some of them, both local Kuwaitis on the outside and foreigners in hiding, all of whom I knew well from projects worked on together. I had a strong sense of, 'There but for the grace of God, went I'.

Since their liberation, on the twenty-sixth of February 1991, as the First Gulf War was coming to an end, the majority of Kuwaitis have become staunch supporters of American military power in the region, hosting significant US forces in their country as a bulwark against subsequent regional trouble. The subsequent failures of the American led coalition in Iraq during and after the Second Gulf War are a secondary consideration to those of their neighbours who suffered at the hand of their erstwhile Iraqi occupiers whom they continue to distrust deeply.

I also recall vividly conversations, both in Kuwait and the UAE with educated Palestinians, doctors, lawyers, architects and the like, whose parents had been persuaded or forced, via displacement from Israeli occupation, to seek a new home in the Gulf. Growing up in affluent Kuwait and speaking the same Arabic mother tongue, would have been significant compensations, but in so many other ways, this diaspora even for the second generation sometimes born abroad rather than in their original homeland, still amounted to dislocation and estrangement.

After the First Gulf War, Palestinians started to be viewed as incomers to Kuwait, and many suffered from a largely unfounded suspicion among the native population that they had been an advance guard for Sadam Hussein's invasion and occupation of the country. Quite how this was supposed to have worked, no one seemed to know, but perception always rides ahead of reality where prejudice is the underlying flavour. After the Iraqis had been expelled by coalition forces, many Palestinians were also forced or preferred to leave Kuwait, no longer feeling welcome. Access to medicine, dentistry and the minutiae of the justice system through accessibly priced trained lawyers became all the poorer as a result, because educated Palestinians who had provided these services had left. I fear the liberating American forces may have had something to do with this second diaspora. Always uncomfortable with the power of educated and eloquent people to spread propaganda against Israel as the strongest ally of the US in the region, anything that disrupted Palestinian welfare seemed like fair game after 1991.

It seems that even when you experience the trauma of losing your homeland, your contribution as an immigrant abroad comes at a price. Sometimes, that price is being forced to move on yet again and perhaps never being allowed to settle. Perhaps forgiveness is the penultimate sentiment to be put back in place when recovering from trauma; trust being the last of all.

Middle East poverty and deprivation

Poverty is perhaps the most debilitating condition to beset mankind and is a type of trauma that knows no limits and little relief. We are blithely told (probably by those who have never experienced the condition) that, "The poor are always with us." Across much of the Middle East, there appears a level of indifference to poverty, as civic awareness and altruism seems at best only to work intermittently even in the richest states, either from government agencies or the more socially conscientious and therefore, charitable mosques and their Imams. There are always exceptions of course. Yet the largest manifestations of poverty, the illegal self-build shanty towns that surround even the wealthiest cities where the poor and otherwise homeless reside, exude a can-do attitude among their inhabitants. Suffering from poverty doubtless exists, but on public display, there is little apparent self-pity.

As part of my understanding of the imperatives of urban development, I have walked the lengths and breadths of several shanty towns from Morocco to Saudi Arabia, and while they were always sobering and often malodorous experiences, they usually left me with a sense of indomitable spirit at large among the inhabitants. Curiosity coupled with invariable politeness have been the usual reactions to a foreigner in their midst. If there are children around, the ice gets broken more easily, because curiosity always gets the better of any sense that visitors are unwelcome.

Sadly, shantytown dwellers invariably feel vulnerable and insecure with the knowledge that their makeshift housing is illegal. They expect it to be torn down without warning by the authorities and they and their families to be moved on. Many may be displaced citizens of another country categorised by that glorious modern euphemism, guest workers. So, hostility is rarely a default response towards visiting strangers who, despite their strangeness, may be in a similar state of just passing through. Suspicion grows perhaps, if visitors are assumed to have some municipal or other establishment role and influence and thus right of access and enquiry. Then, you may be less welcome, yet displays of hostility are still rare; inhabitants have too much at stake to make more enemies. It would be an exaggeration to say you can feel completely safe in an illegal self-built housing neighbourhood, but you are just as likely to be mugged on Main Street as in a poor district. Owing to draconian laws against petty crime, muggings of westerners would be rare anywhere in the Middle East - unless of course it was state sponsored. There is nothing that will sufficiently cope with that.

After the many decades of working and travelling in the Middle East, I conclude that kindness and a welcome to visitors remains as strong as its legends relate. It is the one defiance to autocratic and anti-democratic behaviour by governments that the silent majority can display. To that extent, empathy and human understanding do indeed transcend human suffering and with it, reside our hopes for a better future for one of the most benighted regions of the world that does not deserve the suffering it has experienced for so long.

Vietnam – Same old story, four decades on

In recent years, I have visited two very different countries where past troubles traumatised the people, to be offered brief glimpses of how those who suffered are now dealing with the consequences. In Vietnam, four decades after their war to re-unite the country, I expected to be guided with pride around the tunnel complex north of Ho Chi Minh city (formerly Saigon) where in the 1960s and 1970s, the Viet Cong (VC) hid from aerial bombardment by South Vietnamese and American air and ground forces. The complex is a formidable work of engineering underground, where large numbers of troops and resistance fighters could be accommodated in an underground environment, not seeing daylight for days and weeks on end. The traps set to outwit and deal with encroachment by the anti-communist forces were fiendishly ingenious leading to horrific injuries and slow death to those brave or unwise enough to infiltrate. Even crawling through an example of one of those tunnels – without the mantraps - was an unnerving experience, inviting visitors to smell and feel the claustrophobia without the additional fear of attack from outside. I emerged into the daylight with huge relief after merely minutes below ground.

To my surprise, now that Vietnam is at peace imposed by the victorious communist forces, our guide was scathing in his criticism of the VC and their North Vietnamese allies. Over four decades since the war ended with the defeat and absorption of South Vietnam into a communist governed single country, he recounted the experiences of his father and uncle who had fought as officers in the South Vietnamese army. Lucky enough to survive the war, they were luckier still to have survived the aftermath. Transported to re-education centres initially for six months that turned into six years of incarceration, they were brainwashed and suffered countless punishments from which few of their colleagues emerged alive and sane. No PTSD treatments there, merely the brutal sanctions against those making the mistake of being on the losing side.

When he compared the current regime and what he claimed to be its blatant corruption across every aspect of economic life, with what had gone before 1975, our guide could see no improvement in the lot of the common people. He accepted that the previous South Vietnamese regime had exploited the people and brought about much of the atrocious fate to which the country was later subjected, but he said there was no material difference now, even forty years later, to what had gone before. Vietnam is immeasurably better off than at the end of the war in 1975, but he claimed that this was because capitalism is allowed to thrive provided the people stay out of politics, rigidly maintained on a centrally controlled yet collectivist basis. Quite how this works at the level of macroeconomics, stretches the credibility of commentators more skilled than me. I am sure that Karl Marx would be as confused as I am.

I was astonished at such a frank expression of opinions from inside a regime that prided itself on educating its citizens in the fundamentals of Marxism – from each according to their means, to each according to their needs. I asked why he trusted me not to report such apparent subversion to the authorities and he claimed to be able to judge people well and trust those he judged – even writers. However disturbed the father may have been by his war and post war experiences, the son seemed very level-headed. Time heals – even if it may take a generation to do so.

Anyway, his wife and child had already left the country for a new life in Europe and he would be leaving soon in the next few months. He questioned whether he would be allowed back to see his father again. Such a waste of well-educated polyglot individuals from a country in desperate need of them. Little wonder that Europe, Australasia and North America have been magnets for emigration. Perhaps he was right to leave. Such disillusion is unlikely to remain undiscovered for long by the unyielding authorities that run things there. Yet human understanding to the extent of honest commentary to an apparently trusted recent acquaintance seemed still to be present. That much at least offers hope that empathetic relationships can still exist even despite the difficult historical and political context.

Colombia – Emerging positively from a dark past

A similar brain drain has been experienced in Colombia whose trauma has not been warfare with external forces but internal violent strife over more than four decades between at least three warring factions – the narcotics traffickers (Narcos), the communist inspired and supported Revolutionary Armed Forces of Colombia or F.A.R.C, and the government often in the past implicated with, and infiltrated by, undercover factions from each of the other two. Three-cornered civil wars, like that currently in Syria, are rare but offer numerous twists to the violence and distrust between each of the warring contestants.

A few years ago, FARC and the government came to an uneasy truce, followed by a peace deal, recognising the futility of seemingly endless ideological struggle between them. The government were then blindsided by the people who rejected the deal in a referendum, saying that amnesty for FARC terrorists was too much of a let-off for those who had committed terrible crimes of kidnapping, violence and extortion, an echo of the very crimes committed by the Narcos that inspired the FARC resistance movement in the first place. It proves one immutable thing about violence – that it breeds more of the same, like an ever-tightening spiral, as people find themselves unable to forgive and move on when the suffering is too personal. Who am I to criticise? I would probably do the same.

Yet this precious ceasefire - on the streets at least - between the three factions is largely holding. It is under repeated strain with violence occasionally breaking out to and from those who suffered, now seeking compensation or revenge for past crimes. But compared with the anarchy of previous decades, the great majority of the inhabited country (thus excluding Colombia's Amazon territory and some of the Pacific coast) is now broadly at peace. That is a miracle because, from the depths of the worst violence, it is sometimes possible to chart a way back to relative tranquillity. In Colombia just now that seems to be happening.

The enemies of the ideological opposites of the left-wing FARC and more centrist governments were the narcotics traffickers. Their ruthless application of the capitalist principle of market supply and demand, trafficking ever more potent drugs, rapidly reached international criminal proportions from the early 1970s onwards. The history of drug smuggling into North America, where the best prices were obtainable for cheaply refined cocaine, in turn, derived from easily grown coca leaves, is very well documented elsewhere. But nowadays, the internecine warfare between drug gangs and the government's law enforcers has been driven largely into the shadows in most towns and cities, because of military grade investment and support of government crack downs, including massive support from the US.

Perhaps the greatest source of the decline of drug criminality has been an immutable law of demographics or life expectancy - the sheer loss of life at the apex of each criminal cartel. Carlos Escobar was the most famous and flamboyant of these. But eventually, short life expectancy became his fate like most of the other prominent drug lords involved in the unsparing life of dog-eat-dog by which the gangs imposed their control. As the ordinary people proudly claim in Colombia now, the drug people are either in jail for life or dead because they killed each other. This must be qualified by the fact that there remains a lively drug growing culture in the remote and inaccessible parts of the country's Amazon departments. Colombia has yet to liberate its most inaccessible region from the grip of the narco-criminals.

Medellin was widely seen through the 1980s and 1990s as the capital of drug culture in terms of gangs overseeing the growing, refining and transport of highly valued cocaine and worse. It is now a very different city. Neighbourhoods or barrios like Comuna 13 had been no-go areas for anyone other than gangs, paramilitaries, or heavily armed police. Off limits to outsiders or most law enforcers only a few years ago, these barrios are now exemplars of social regeneration. The first catalysts of the sea-change have been a relatively pure form of war weariness, invariably led by women, some of whom added an intriguing sex boycott for their criminally inclined partners. Investment in physical infrastructure and a slow but eventually overwhelming change in the style and purpose of graffiti followed, but perhaps this most intimate of domestic sanctions was the most effective.

The sex boycott was a fascinating example that violence can be combated psychologically as well as militarily. In a macho culture, ridicule must be avoided at all costs, not to mention cross-legged frustration. Less flamboyant examples of public shaming have proved similarly effective – the calling out of bad driving habits by public display of those convicted for example. It is odd that we consider people's human rights to have been violated if they are seen to be punished in public. Excess pride ('The law can't touch me!') is the common failing of many petty criminals, so that if punishment included public shaming, many might stop short of committing the crime in the first place. The principle of the mediaeval stocks may yet have a place in society.

More concrete examples of regeneration in Medellin have arrived in the last ten years, by installing electric escalators in poor residential barrios or neighbourhoods, enabling relatively safe access to and from steep hillside housing to schools and centres of employment. There is also now an elaborate cable car network linked to the equally iconic city-wide metro system that has transformed accessibility between parts of the city and thus safer commuting to and from school and places of work. Having worked for many city authorities seeking to install new infrastructure, I have nothing but admiration for those who achieve it and reap the social benefits. These are profound.

Graffiti has been the most visual inspiration of regenerated morale, as it evolved from a medium of protest with attendant violent and negative imagery, transforming into images of hope and optimism. Now, the best street artists are at work all over the city, painting positive images of birds and plants – images of natural life and family-based communities just living out their existences, still poor but with hope and a positive pre-disposition for the future. There is a strong feminist strain to this as well - pushback against male-dominated machismo breeding violence through excess pride and the fear of ridicule. We should adopt such tactics in our inner cities in Europe and North America as well.

This characteristic of positivism is critical. Colombians are mainly outward looking, welcoming and oh-so-friendly to strangers. They may have endured decades of psychopathic behaviour across their communities, but the great majority have put this behind them, and they look to the future positively as they emerge from their dark past. This is an object lesson to communities in the rest of the world enduring similar, if differently sourced, troubles; to be optimistic that there are better times ahead. Some gain their inspiration for this from religious conviction, but for this to succeed, I believe that there needs to be a strong humanist spirit underlying faith. Colombians have got that in very large measure and they thoroughly deserve their better times.

Bereavement

Bereavement is probably the deepest, most private and longest lasting of the traumatic human conditions. We come into this world alone with a little help – sometimes a lot - from our mothers whom we have yet to get to know. Later, we leave in a similar way – on our own. In the intervening period, most of us gain an understandable impression that life only works properly as a partnership with family, friends and colleagues, who share with us apparently common experience of triumph, disaster, joys, let downs, euphoria and depression and every other impostor to our senses in between.

But are we really anything more than individual entities passing through life on our own? The sense of bereavement when a loved one or even a mere friend or acquaintance dies, suggests otherwise, that we need others to give our lives meaning beyond mere existence. So, the trauma of losing others is acute at the time, and, in my experience, never leaves. A thick carapace grows over the raw wound of loss but pick away at it or scrape it off altogether through memories either happy or sad, and the wound of loss is still there. We remember the person that is no longer with us realising that their presence had and still has contributed to our true sense of being. It is a strange sentiment that we never fully appreciate what we have, until we have it no more. The company of loved ones is the most precious of these losses.

#BeKind and Maslow's hierarchy of needs

Back with my chapter theme – does coping with bereavement and war, physical pain from a medical condition, collective fear of violence or social upheaval, poverty or rejection make us any more empathetic in our connections with others? Strangely, given the general tenor of this title, I think not. Everything is contextual, as I will explore in a following chapter. I think such experiences can make us more compassionate, but compassion is not the same as empathy. I can feel compassion for you, or you for me, but it may not be reciprocated. Compassion can work as a one-way street; empathy needs an exchange of emotions.

Empathy or the generation of meaningful connections with other people is a lot more about mutuality. That is perhaps the wellspring of the recent #BeKind movement. Quite apart from the benefits to the receiver, actively seeking opportunities for being kind to people gives a warm feeling to the sender. This must be applied with caution. I am not sure that the #BeKind movement adequately reflects the need for understanding between individuals and the deeper sense of connection that this requires. It takes time to make such connections so is not available for every encounter, but a kind thought, or deed is a great start.

I doubt that real understanding between two people can be achieved unless and until both parties have some sense of feeling of what the other is experiencing. We are all individuals after all. Maslow's hierarchy is well enough known these days with its five tiers from the most basic human needs such as food, water, warmth and rest, then safety and security, all the way up to self-fulfilment and achieving one's full potential in life including creativity. Commencing meaningful connections between people is probably dependent on the two levels of need in the middle of the hierarchy, where a sense of belonging and love at the third level may graduate to the fourth, where self-esteem emerges. Without this critical aspect of self-appraisal, it is unlikely that sufficient self-confidence exists with which to engage meaningfully with other people.

Empathy at least provides you or me with the means to relate to each other on the basis that we have some sense of each other's innermost feelings. This is a precious sentiment that, found between previous strangers, is one of the most rewarding of bases for understanding the human condition. We are not alone in the world despite our arrivals and departures seeming to make it so, and our sense of self-worth and belonging is utterly bound up in our relationships. There is nothing more fundamental to connecting with others than realising this and living our lives together as one of the eternal verities of a happy existence. That is one ultimate victory over trauma, perhaps the best. Time – but also good relationships – heal.

Chapter 6

Homeland Loves and Hates

Our love of where we come from sometimes dressed up as patriotism and sometimes nationalism, can create negativity in how we relate to our fellow citizens and those of other nations.

*

My book has so far broadly assumed that meaningful connections are either made or not, only between fellow humans. These connections are engendered (or not) between at least two people who have a higher level of communication between them identified by intelligent anticipation of how each of them think and react to the other. One of the main indicators of empathy being present in a relationship is the capacity to alter mood and behaviour to match different circumstances.

But can empathy be engendered through an individual's identification with place? And if presented with the evidence of a love of place, does that make those thus affected more susceptible to meaningful connections with their fellow human beings?

There is plenty of evidence of peoples' love of place – their identification with somewhere that generates positive feelings and occasionally the opposite, such as sadness or melancholy, but still perhaps based on love. Such emotions are particularly prevalent for people who live a long way (either in terms of distance or culture) from where they were brought up or lived through significant times in their life. If the memories engendered were happy, the moods generated will probably be happy too, perhaps tinged with melancholy, a yearning for what is past and never to be recovered. The Welsh language has a word for this that does not translate easily to English – hiraeth. We are a nostalgic lot.

If a place is identified with broadly negative memories, then the reaction will likely be similarly negative, and most would choose not to re-visit. Yet, even here, there are exceptions - satisfaction at having put sadness aside replaced by a feeling that a place no longer holds fears of association. So, positives and negatives in equal measure but all induced by a response to place not people.

This is probably more complex stuff than I realise and there are no hard and fast rules. Current circumstances will also determine reactions to place. If my mood is bright, my memories of a place will likely reflect that, if melancholy, likewise. Place in these circumstances is merely the backdrop to mood, and empathy may not arise.

A good helping of chauvinism is built-in to people's love of place, suggesting that the location itself is merely the excuse to promote other feelings - of pride, patriotism, love of nature, awareness of a social condition and so on. Yet, I am convinced that in the still small voice of calm that accompanies the deepest and probably most private reflections, a sense of place can be expressed as empathy, reflected back if not on the inanimate location itself, then on the people encountered there or thereafter.

My own love of place is centred round its uniqueness to me, and that implies a relatively remote location, not frequented by many. Anything more commonly visited would mean multiple other impressions would also exist, clouding the personal ones and diluting the sense that this is my own and no one else's feeling. I accept that others may empathise with a place precisely because they feel the same as me about it. But for me, perhaps like my religious feelings, it is the personal that counts more than the collective, because the voice of the God to whom I can relate is only heard by me through silence, not collective gatherings or worship. A place, and for that matter, a concept of the divine, only grows on me through quiet reflection.

So where are these places that mean so much? And will I destroy their uniqueness to me by revealing them to you? There is little point in others seeking out my empathetic places because mood, memory, and circumstance at the time when the place was exalted to special status will always be unique to each individual. My purpose in listing favourite places generating my sense of empathy is to encourage others to go seek or express their own, not to experience mine. G'wan, go find your own, if you don't already know where they are.

First off, there are some places for me that can never induce a real sense of connection. Big cities have too much noise and hyper-activity going on to generate anything beyond keeping your wits about you, knowing where you are headed and finding a way through the crowds. Lots of entertainment value, I grant, including inspiring theatre, art, music and the regeneration of places breathing new life and vibrancy to the communities thus supported. But none of this represents love of place, merely place as a means to an end.

So, my current home city of London like many other metropoles, has lots to recommend it, especially to keep me on my toes and younger than I might be in more tranquil settings. But that does not represent any real connection. Much more reflective responses are needed, before empathy rises.

Pembrokeshire my county

The most obvious place with which I and perhaps others from similarly iconic places, feel empathy, is my birthplace and place of growing up. Pembrokeshire is my long-lost home county that

I left many times to go to school and college, but to which I returned, like a homing pigeon, for over two decades always on the move aged between the ages of ten and thirty. Now visits are less frequent, but all the more poignant and treasured for that rarity.

Being the end of a peninsula, the road and rail lines help a lot to build Pembrokeshire's uniqueness; you cannot go any further west, south or north without swimming, so its human umbilical is only eastwards. That axial relationship with neighbours near and far is one of many geographical features that appeal. If land boundaries connect you to people and culture on the other side of them, sea boundaries connect you with the infinite – that greater part of our planet where man is out of his element and where nature alone determines the circumstances of travel. There is virtually no 'being' at sea; humans are always going somewhere or having to do something in that element.

Geography alone cannot generate empathy. If so, everywhere would have a claim because everywhere is unique geographically. For me, a critical factor is memories – of long or short walks over fields, cliffs and valleys, sailings via rough or calm sea passages, parties held in particular places or just mooning about night or day feeling the earth beneath your feet when standing, or under your back and legs when lying flat out on it and staring straight up at the sky, light, dark or starlit. I did a fair part of that when young, being something of a dreamer.

Islands also have a special appeal to me. Separation is always a good start in the search for empathy. Rather like those occasional misfits at school, I am drawn to otherness, and the otherness of islands from their proximal mainland, probably appeals to a contrarian streak in my nature.

Combining the two categories above, my birthplace county is surrounded on three sides by sea, with an indented coastline and the most diverse physical and historical structures found in any single county of Britain. The whole geological table from Pre-Cambrian to the Paleontological Age is represented here, and the place names reference Welsh, Norse, Flemish, French and most recently English as the languages of choice. Cultures are a bit more complicated to define; one of the place's special appeals.

Surprisingly, given nearly one hundred and fifty miles of indented coastline, Pembrokeshire has only a handful of islands, some inhabited, such as Caldey off the little Regency town of Tenby, where Cistercian monks and a few farmers still live off the balmy southern climate growing flowers to make perfumes; Skomer, with its bird sanctuary including the county's National Park symbol, the humorous Puffin; and Ramsey, with one farm accessed by a wild crossing from the St Justinian's lifeboat station near St David's. But the uninhabited ones - Skokholm, Grassholm, and the Smalls, with their lonely automatic light, twenty miles out into the Atlantic, are more fascinating - the remoter the better.

An island love affair

Before I turn this into a travel guide, I had better reduce it to the personal realm. For a fourteen-year-old with occasional pubescent dreams of inhabiting his own private space, there was one smaller island within reach, with the uninspiring name of Stack Rocks, about a mile off the coast at St Brides and two from my favourite seaside village of Little Haven. One warm summer day in 1965 (there were a few, honestly), I persuaded my elder cousin Doug, who's much-loved and tinkered over small boat Lucy had a 3HP 2 stroke outboard engine, to make a trip and plant a flag. He seemed to prefer spending time in the boatyard, constantly repairing the engine, but I persuaded him that day to mount an exhibition to Stack. This was an hour's sailing time at Lucy's maximum speed. The sun was high, hardly a cloud in the sky and the sea was - unusually - millpond calm. Time to go.

I had prepared my flag declaring UDI. Unilateral Declarations of Independence were in fashion that year, after the style of Rhodesia, so I thought it suitable for my Republic of Stack. Human Population: occasional; Seabird Population: too numerous to count and as we found out, aggressive; source of Gross National Product: guano or bird shit. Stack is two blocks of rock about forty metres high connected by a lower causeway, all of it about one hundred metres long and fifty metres, at its widest, so not big enough to sustain independence. But big enough for dreams.

We landed on the modest high tide swell in the one small sea inlet and tying Lucy fore and aft, we climbed up through thick plantains to the island's summit. I planted my flag with due ceremony, watched by some puzzled seals in the sea below and the island's entire colony of disturbed seagulls, cormorants and gannets. Gannets were so common off the Welsh coasts at that time, that the 'Min of Ag and Fish' as they were known, would pay you a shilling for each one you killed, as they ate their own weight in fish every day. Doubtless gannets are now protected, but mackerel have no voice in Parliament.

Views that day were long and clear in all directions; thirty kilometres to the north across St Brides Bay to the St David's peninsula, south to the nearby St Brides village, a mile away with its then derelict Kensington isolation hospital (now a high end spa resort), and two miles eastwards back to Little Haven, where we would soon be regaling the pub locals with tales of derring-do. But out to the west, there was almost nothing, except the seaward horizon, the western Atlantic, in its most rare and benign state: Grassholm, twelve miles west and the remotest of all Trinity House lighthouses on the Smalls (still manned in the 1960s) a further eight miles west again and just visible on this clearest of days.

At times like this, I tended to daydream of what was to come; storms lashing the coast, the wind strong enough to carry foam off the top of each wave and the seagulls driven before it like so much flying flotsam; no weather for venturing out in small boats such as ours. But this was high summer, calm seas and warm weather, so why could I not continue being a will-o'-the-wisp dreamer, listening to the waves lapping the rocks, the seagulls' call with the soft warm wind ruffling the thin grass on the summit? My own special island.

We waited half an hour for the Air-Sea rescue helicopter from RNAS Brawdy to come and check us out, perhaps accompanied by Interpol to arrest us for the treasonous declaration of independence. But eventually, growing bored at the world's indifference, we made our way home to Little Haven, trailing a mackerel line unrewarded by an evening catch. The next year, 1966, I went back and there was, of course, no sign of my flag, blown away landward on the first winter gale where someone would have wondered at its strange incomprehensible message But amazingly, my bamboo flag pole was still there, slightly chewed by a curious bird but just about upright offering little resistance to the wind. I was proud of that.

Thus, ended my first island love affair, leaving me with fascination for remote places, most of which have offered slightly more human stimulus than Stack. Motivated by pure nostalgia and boyhood memories, I have been back there in recent years. Not much has changed; thicker vegetation, smellier guano, fewer gannets (the fish must be pleased) and no seals to be seen, but no flagpole either after nearly forty years. My Republic rests merely in memory and imagination but it is a generator of empathy as strong as any human relationship.

Remoteness induces melancholy

Another island that invokes a special, if fleeting, sense of attachment could not be further from the first. It is so remote that I am unlikely ever to visit again. That is part of its appeal, there is a special melancholy – hiraeth - about a place you know you will never see again. Paradoxically, it almost strengthens a sense of belonging, as if witness of its continued existence will be left to others with similar attachment. And belonging is a consensual emotion where connection with others is an integral part of it.

Set in the middle of the South Pacific Ocean is the French territory of Nouvelle Caledonie, a two hundred-kilometre by forty-kilometre island, large by typical island dimensions in the Pacific. Immediately to its south lies the Ile des Pins, an ex-penal colony during the last part of the nineteenth and the early twentieth centuries. Now, it is a sparsely inhabited place of some twenty kilometres in diameter and its Kanak indigenous population are related to their fellow Melanesians in faraway Tahiti. They are now mixed with French stock some of whom are descendants of the criminals expelled from the French metropole, never to return at the end of their sentences because of the enormous distances involved. Its social history serves to emphasise its remoteness.

There was one-way home for the convicts in 1914, to join a punishment battalion of the rapidly expanding French army facing German invasion. For the very few who even survived the next four-year holocaust of death and injury, there was a mandate that they should return to complete their sentences. It is not known whether their period of army service was included or excluded from their periods of sentence, but given that all other males of a qualifying age were also called up, it is unlikely that four years would have been taken off their terms. Harsh times marked by a forlorn war memorial to the dead of the First

World War. In 1924, the penal colony was disbanded but faced with the expense of their return passage to France, the pitiful few left by the end, had little choice but to stay. They intermarried with local women and a mixed-race population grew up, as for similar miscegenation on the larger island of New Caledonia to the north.

Such melancholic human stories helped to colour my mood when visiting there. But even Ile des Pins does not represent the special place I have chosen as invoking this empathy in me. On the last day of our trip, we took a boat ride out to desert islands and tidal sand cays away to the south. Sea eagles nested on rocky promontories and huge skuas that glide for hundreds of miles across the ocean vastness, were especially invocative of the remoteness, So too, were the sea turtles, tame enough or rather sensing no fear, to swim up close to our boat, going nose-to-nose with those who dived to swim with them.

The boat's captain and his crew comprised his wife and lively six-year-old daughter. He decided without consulting us, to drop us on a tidal sand cay about half a mile long and a few yards wide, to go to another island and prepare a barbecue. We were out of sight of other land and the width of the sand cay seemed to be getting narrower still as the tide encroached. As their boat disappeared over the horizon, I wondered idly whether we would see them again, but we had not paid them anything yet and had our money and cameras with us, so we assumed all would be well. There were a few dried out and long dead trees clinging to the higher parts of the cay, but not even enough to afford a sun-shade canopy - just the sound of the small wavelets edging the brilliant turquoise sea and the brightest of white sand in the clearest air imaginable so far from man-made pollutants. It is strange what warm sun and lapping seawater can do to your general sense of wellbeing.

Our boatman duly returned after half an hour with his small crew, and sensing our relief, took us on to a larger island about two kilometres long and one hundred metres wide with dense vegetation and convenient shade across its middle. They had prepared the promised barbecue of delicious fish with rice and salad, shared with a small group of Japanese honeymooners who had arrived on another boat - as you do, these tourist-driven days - in the middle of the trackless Pacific.

We were presented with the largest lobster we had ever seen. It was over a metre long and over ten kilos in weight – known locally as a Porcelaine because of its brilliant bone china colouring. It was apparently dead and pronounced too old and tough to eat, so likely to become a trophy on the boatman's wall at home. We were horrified when it went back into a very large bucket and started moving around, lightly flipping its enormous tail.

The boatman's little girl scampered off into the undergrowth and came back holding by the tail, a small black and white striped snake called a tricotier because of its resemblance to one of those pullovers from far away France. She seemed completely fearless as she swung it around. They have poison in their bite but have such small teeth and jaws, they can only do you damage if they bite you in the soft webbing between the fingers. So that was all right then. Luckily, the little girl's mother also thought her behaviour with the snake was at least disrespectful and persuaded her to let it go. It slithered off into the low vegetation, on which we kept a close eye for the rest of the meal.

Returning from that boat trip seemed like returning from the very ends of the earth with the sea breeze and bright sunlight sustaining a warm sense of wellbeing. Remote places have a peculiar quality of melancholy if you sense that you will never go back. Parting even from places as well as people is a sweet sorrow and it invokes in me a deep sense of empathy for places in the world like our special desert isle. Out of sight and direct touch of most of mankind, such places are left peculiarly vulnerable to the worst excesses that our indifferent but often lethal species can impose on nature.

Here was an almost unspoilt wilderness of sea and occasional tiny islands where turtles were still fearless enough to swim nose to nose with humans, where the coral was so dark red or pearly white and healthy and the tropical fish which depended on it, swam unaware of the dangers of climate warming already slowly impacting this precious space. It made me sad to recall its suffering fellow species closer to civilisation a few hundred miles to the west on Australia's Great Barrier Reef, where, we are told, higher sea temperatures have already killed off so much of the delicate ecosystem only two metres below the surface.

My empathy here was undoubtedly with place, and definitely not with humankind, because despite their invisibility, the forces of our uncaring exploitation of the planet we share with the flora and fauna there, were already encroaching on this mini paradise. Leaving the little island behind, where we had eaten our barbecue, left me with an acute melancholy. I will never go back and anyway, it may never be the same, unless we change our behaviours radically.

A sense of place through animism
One of the most moving experiences of empathy with nature, if not a specific place, that I have encountered was in the Masai Mara game reserve in Kenya. John, our guide was a natural savanna bushman with a calm demeanour and natural dignity that reassured us that we were in good hands. He spoke with quiet matter-of-factness about the mission school that he had attended as a child, where those professing Christian faith were

given lunch, while those who did not or would not, went hungry or had to bring their own food. He did not seem to be the sort to be making it up, but he and his parents stuck to their animist beliefs and he went hungry until he got home.

There are many variants of this inner calm, but in John's part of east Africa, it often takes the form of finding his God in the natural world of animals, plants, landscape and sky. His tranquillity and quiet commentaries on the wild game both big and small that he found for us were exciting and calming in equal measure. He afforded as much time and, it seemed, loving knowledge, to the lower order of species including the much-derided hyenas. He conveyed a sense of the cycles of wildlife, birth and death and the times before and after each as well, that seemed to retain their own constant rhythm.

One day, he took us for a walk through the bush savanna that, as active lion country seemed a risky venture. His only apparent defence was a long assegai spear, though I suspect there were other guides on call by handset should we encounter serious threats. He described how one of his rites of passage to Masai manhood was to go hunting a lion that had been taking cattle from his father's kraal, armed only with a similar spear. At sixteen or seventeen, that must have been daunting, but the quiet account of how he had killed the offending big cat suggested there was no exaggeration. We completed our bush walking tour without incident, the wildflowers forming as much of his commentary as anything more attention seeking on four or two legs.

While driving in John's bush vehicle, several miles distant from our campsite and other guided parties with their own vehicles, we encountered a lone bull elephant, lighter grey and even a partly dusty pink with age, the possessor of only one long tusk. He was following another family group of elephants but at about a mile distant. John explained that this ageing bull had probably been rejected from the larger group by its matriarch, but he was refusing to break contact. We stopped at what we thought was a respectful distance to watch his movements, flicking dust over his shoulders in a manner that immediately implied frustration with his lot. But then he turned his attention to our vehicle that had encroached on his already challenged territory and pawed the ground hard with his giant ears flapping. He was the picture of agitation even to an untutored eye.

John wisely decided to move off, but at the critical moment, the car's gears jammed, and we were stuck where we were with the elephant getting more and more angry at our intrusion. Displaying only a small margin more concern, John told us to stay very still with no talking even within the vehicle. Very slowly, he took out a long thin metal whistle and blew long and hard into it, to no apparent audible effect to our hearing. But a very high-pitched note that we could not register, was received by the elephant well enough. He did not like it at all and turning, lumbered off in a cloud of dust together with a further dent to his fading dignity.

Other guides and vehicles were summoned by radio and with a rare display of rifle firepower surrounding us, everyone jumped out to examine the car's inner workings deeming them to be beyond repair in the bush. We were towed back to camp feeling a little deflated – a bit like the elephant perhaps. But John's relief at the safe outcome of this incident centred mainly around the voluntary departure of the bull. The dignity of this old, proud animal had been much reduced by circumstances, but his life, such as would be left of it, was spared.

I believe that John was so in touch with the natural world that he inhabited that it would be quite appropriate to say that he was in total empathy with it. He was rightly proud of his Masai warrior heritage, but he was even more a living part of where he lived; just one more species among the many. Not everyone could make claim to his beliefs and I have no hard evidence of his happy condition. He just exuded quiet confidence without any excessive display of overt pride; one of nature's gentlemen by any definition, content within his own skin, clearly a lover of place alongside any humanity.

Patriotism games

Another love of place amounts to patriotism or love of one's country – as distinct from nationalism that seems to me to amount to the loathing of all others. How can love of place be projected onto such a wide canvas as a country? Even the most starry-eyed accept that there is bad as well as good in all societies, though some patriots might argue that dealing with the negatives in their own country is part of any love affair with it. 'They may be negatives but they are my negatives!' might be the trope, while, 'My country, right or wrong' seems to be a nationalist rather than patriotic meme.

I suppose that patriotism is also filled with hope or aspiration – that your country or society will prove somehow to be greater than the sum of its parts. In Britain's imperial, that is to say, expansionary times, that was easy enough to understand, but such sentiments are widely reviled nowadays because of the costs to those colonised or otherwise exploited. Now, we might seek out a softer power influence for our country, that it should be a force for good in the world, a protector of personal liberty, an upholder of democratic tradition and a pursuer after truth. Do we shape up? All of these and many other higher ideals are under attack as my first and second chapters partly addressed, but that does not stop the patriot from hoping that we can achieve more good in the world than harm.

There must be some powerful empathy at work within the concept of patriotism because acts of bravery or sacrifice in war and in response to the suffering of others, implies a powerful loyalty of sorts. Armies have thought this through, and the idea of Queen and Country or whatever other national icons apply, counts for them much less than, 'Standing by your mates'. This explains their deployment of small fighting units where individuals can relate to each other and a sense of loyalty is engendered towards the common cause. No matter, if the common cause is surviving the mission and bringing your mates through with you, it is still an effective source of collective action and maintaining morale. If army psychologists can be as dispassionate as this in analysing how soldiers might act extraordinarily and selflessly in danger, it follows that we should examine patriotism rigorously to avoid any humbug. Can love of place in this wider sense survive as an idea or is it really love of something more conceptual than concrete?

Some societies challenge the patriotic mantra, accusing it of being a plot to disguise crimes at a collective national scale by those charged with committing them. 'A flag is just a piece of cloth', I read once during an anti-nationalist demonstration in Barcelona. That might work at the intellectual level – in fact, it is indisputable in a literal sense. But try abusing a country's flag in front of its citizens and watch identity turn into collective disapproval or worse. We all relate to somewhere or to something and while it is almost impossible to define what makes for loyalty to a country, it is probably a sense of irreducible homeland that is playing to the emotions. These days, with so much transparency about human behaviour, the simple idea of homeland is likely to resonate far more with people than any attempt to suggest that one country's moral values are superior to any others.

Germany is a country that fascinates me for what I would describe as post nationalist values, found among most of the population, at least until a few years ago. So awful had been the

Nazis' crimes against humanity, still within living memory of older Germans, that their post war generations made it a material act of will, including wholesale revision of school curricula, to start coming to terms with the wrong doings of that recent past. Widespread acceptance of this history was by no means a given, despite overwhelming evidence. We have seen too many examples of human denial elsewhere in recent years to know that it would have been far from easy to acknowledge past crimes.

But to German society's enormous credit, the awful past has been absorbed into the collective psyche with a consequent reappraisal of the nature of pride in country, patriotism, or nationalism. Rather than present their own kind as uniquely evil that would have been both implausible and deeply damaging to national self-awareness, the German educational authorities emphasised the fallibility of all human nature. To me, this taught German children some unpalatable truths about human nature, to which other nationalities have not yet been adequately exposed. For me, that is a far more honest education about human weakness than for example, British equivalent re-appraisal of our colonial past. This is not to decry British colonialism out of hand, though many do just that these days, but rather to look at past history dispassionately with no tinted spectacles presuming that we were largely on the side of good while the others were not.

Precisely because Britain came through the last world war victorious as the only protagonist with Nazism and its Japanese equivalent that was there from start to finish of declared warfare, a myth has been allowed to take hold about our own heroic nature. True, the contribution to victory was steadfast and long lasting but it was not the greatest. Two more populous countries, the (then) Soviet Union and the US must battle it out figuratively, for such honours, merely reflecting their larger scale and in the case of the former, their greater suffering and loss of life. While there is justifiable pride in the British contribution to defeating fanatical autocracy, it has also left some of us with a belief in our own permanent rightness of purpose and incorruptible rectitude. For me, that falls well within the bounds of nationalism and is not patriotic at all. Indeed, I resent deeply those of a jingoistic nature who claim our national virtues as their own monopoly on patriotism. They are armchair patriots.

If there was a patriotic strain in German rebuilding of their moral compass after the war, it was based on an understanding of the weakness in all human nature and their need to rise above it. They did that specifically through objective support for hunting down their war criminals but more generally, eschewing previous tendencies to see things through the prism of purely national interest. As our world gets smaller through ever greater connectivity, so we all need to embrace this philosophy of post nationalism that Germany may have started to build. Indeed, we could boost the advancement of the concept, by adopting it in our own historical curricula before even the Germans begin to lose it to more nationalistic sentiments that have raised their hydra heads among their far-right supporters in recent years.

Post nationalism would embrace the principle that no country has a moral superiority over others and that given the right context and circumstances, barbarous acts committed by one group, could have been committed by any other group, regardless of nationality. Barbarity is a human behaviour characteristic as much as love and nurture. I am not sure that we British are yet capable of accepting that, maintaining a belief in our own past and future nobility to rise above such extreme behaviour. But if we do not accept that truth about human nature, we do ourselves the disservice of damaging misrepresentation of our potential selves. The best way to behave well on the world stage is to understand the potential for doing the opposite.

So, there are definite limits to my sense of empathy through place. It only extends to patriotism as a fleeting and passing sense of pride imposed by a temporary upper hand in sport or other competitive endeavour. I must, therefore, qualify my opening hypothesis that a sense of connection and empathy is engendered by place. This only really works at the entirely individual level when perceiving a homeland. Once it becomes a collective sense, it is susceptible to dangerous politics outside individual control.

But that does not stop me yearning for my small island paradise far away to the west on the edge of 'my' country and county. It is still there in my dreams and that perhaps is where a love of place should stay.

Chapter 7

Judgement in Context

Context determines almost all our judgement faculties when assessing any fresh situation or behaviour pattern as we forge new relationships. Looking at familiar situations from a fresh viewpoint shows how critical context is to any encounter or discussion and the likely outcome of new friendships.

*

When seeking solutions for fractured relationships that now dominate so much of society, context is a pretty good place to start. Developing new ways of receiving, understanding, interpreting and responding to signals or messages coming our way can shift us to a better approach to the resulting dialogue. It will also give us a better prospect of establishing rapport and empathy when we engage with others.

I am never sure which is the more engaging activity; hearing or listening. Both imply that audio signals are being received but listening is no better a guarantee of understanding than mere hearing. 'I hear you', is supposed to mean that I understand what you are telling me, better perhaps than just listening, but still listening gives a stronger impression that the whole of a message is being absorbed. Simon and Garfunkel's song, *The Sound of Silence* captured this when they sang about people 'hearing without listening', but could it equally have been the other way around?

Whatever. One myth buster to consider: neither hearing nor listening are passive processes. We are encouraged to believe that speaking is active while listening is passive, but proper listening is anything but passive. It requires a high level of engagement with what is being said, to receive it as closely to what the speaker is trying to say before interpreting it for one's own comprehension. This is demanding stuff because far too many of us tend to be forming an opinion of what is being said before we have even heard the end of the first sentence. This is understandable in the world of time banditry that some speakers adopt (politicians are past masters) in order to reduce the time for any damaging rebuttal or even simple dialogue. But really, to be as objective as possible about what we hear, we should try to take in what we are being told before processing it to form an opinion, for, against or in some way qualifying the message.

Never mind the message, who is the messenger?
A consequence of this early opinion forming about what we hear (I know I am guilty), is asking myself as I am hearing a message, "Wait up! Who is telling me this?" In the era of frequent fake news and its subtler cousin, fake interpretation, we now process the source as readily as we do the message. The old phrase, "Well, THEY would say that, wouldn't they!" has never been more apt as a reaction to the latest breaking news or titillating rumour. Which political spectrum you come from will invariably colour your reaction to stuff you hear – either to believe it if from a trusted source, or to dismiss it, if not. Little room for context in the middle.

Much of this cynical response to what we hear – believing some and rejecting the rest almost regardless of content – is more prevalent when hearing media broadcasts or reading stuff online. Face-to-face, there are different dynamics in play. An essential part of achieving understanding with others is both to listen to them and fully hear what they are saying, in order to judge them and what they say more effectively. Touchy feely thinking uses phrases like, "I empathise with you," or the more cloying, "I feel your pain." But empathy, like proper listening, is very far from the passive process that these sorts of sentiment imply. Empathetic understanding, that I have also defined as imaginative identification, goes a lot further towards anticipating what someone is thinking or doing even before they speak. To act before having to be asked is part of identifying imaginatively with others.

Far too few of us are good listeners and because there is no listening involved in digital (a.k.a. written) communications, these become a series of monologues rather than proper dialogue. I write a carefully crafted message to you and you write one back. No real absorption of each other's opinion needed in any of that. This type of exchange has diminished our skills in responding to people based on what they are telling us in favour of sticking to a previously defined script of our own. I notice this among some younger people for whom conversational discourse with anyone other than their immediate friends, is a bit intimidating. Maybe, it is just me displaying characteristics of an older and more cantankerous generation? But two-way conversations with some younger people whom I do not know well, are often quite difficult when they lack the filter of a handheld device.

The loss of spontaneity in conversation

Millennials and younger generations than them are of course the ones who have been most exposed to digital forms of communication having grown up with them. Digital communication gives time to think before responding. This might lend a new quality to conversation but not everyone uses the extra time wisely. More important, the spontaneity of instant dialogue is lost when you cannot see as well as hear, rather than read, the other person's response. Maybe again, it is just me, but I always have an underlying impression that what people write even in a WhatsApp message, is still very much considered and curated more than is ever possible with face-to-face speech. And some of it is out-and-out narcissistic. Pity the loss of impressions based on facial expression. And I do not mean an emoji.

To apply a little empathy to you my unknown reader, I imagine you asking, "What is wrong with thinking before responding?" Certainly, it is true that most of us have been guilty of engaging mouth before brain, but spontaneity is an essential part of getting to know people. Digital communicators cannot fully replace spontaneity and they rule out observation of body language. We need to be fully aware of these shortcomings.

It is not only visual impression that provides colour to individual relationships. Surrounding context or mood is just as important – happy or carefree being one example, menacing and scary entirely another. Between these two extremes lies a lot of ambient context that can determine our memories of things more than the mere events themselves. The mood of the person you are speaking to is also conveyed immediately when you are face-to-face. Body language rather than what is said can invariably convey more and the way we engage with each other, is subconsciously adjusted for the perception of mood. Very little of this is available when communicating digitally, which is perhaps, why some digital messages get wrongly interpreted or end up in a slanging match. It may not have been the content of the exchange that sparked this off but rather the tone – and context. Mood is critical to context.

Let me offer a little example from my youth. On trying to teach me good cricket shots, or some other sporting skill, my dad would say to me, "Do what I say, not what I do." I would have put this down to hypocrisy if I had not seen the twinkle in his eye. That told me a lot more than the simple words, in other words, "We are all inconsistent, but I am telling you the theory.

Stick with that as best you can." Now try writing that in an email or WhatsApp message. It will surely not work. Where is the twinkle?

Context is also crucial to how we perceive experiences, whether positively, negatively or nuanced from anywhere in between. If we are feeling open and receptive to new impressions, they are far more likely to go down well than if we are feeling slightly grumpy, under the weather or just sad. So much valuable experience is lost if we are negatively exposed to it; so much can be gained even from the most unpromising circumstances if our pre-disposition is more positive.

Gaining from a personal crisis in India

I am reminded of an incident several years ago in India that neatly illustrates this point. It first appears as a major personal disaster but slowly reveals itself as a wonderful opportunity to study diverse human natures on show. Valuable stuff for a writer about fractured society, but it needs a bit of background context for you to get the full picture. Bear with me.

Arriving by train at Delhi's main railway station, I became the victim of a well-choreographed pickpocket routine. Chasing after the porter who had seized my bag off the high-level luggage rack, I did not spot, or rather feel, the lifting of passport and mobile phone from my zipped-up backpack. (Travellers tip: loss from pockets rather than bags is usually sensed more quickly.) The next morning, the British High Commission offered tea, brief sympathy for a common occurrence and an all-important temporary, cream, cardboard passport with which to seek a new entry visa from Indian Immigration. Without this, I would not have been able to leave India in ten days' time. If you had not arrived, how could you be allowed to depart? Kafka-esque or what?

Visiting the inland office of the Indian Immigration Service was initially a descent into bureaucratic purgatory but turned into a wonderful opportunity to observe human behaviour in all its variety. In a hall the size of an aircraft hangar, hundreds of foreigners of every description were queuing for emergency visas. Many had been victims far worse than me, including violent muggings. Rendered penniless and devoid of ID, some had been forced to beg lifts over long distances to Delhi, one of the few places where their identity could be re-instated. The need to recount these experiences to casual listeners either willing or otherwise, was part of victim recovery therapy.

Around the hall's perimeter, there was a series of desks numbered one to twenty, each representing a separate bureaucratic stage towards identity re-instatement, ending with the nirvana of re-possessing a stamped entry visa. This final accolade would be bestowed by the boss of the whole system, magnificently named on a sign hanging above his slightly elevated desk, 'InCharge' (all one word). We were in for a long haul.

I started badly, having completed the initial registration form by hand, only to have it politely rejected – "not completed 'online!" How was I supposed to do this? 'Online, outside – outside!" I was quickly directed to the solution that represented for me the perfect metaphor for the modern Indian condition – crippling public sector bureaucracy and a lively adjacent private enterprise sector ready to respond. For the price of a soda, a samosa and a ten-rupee fee, a soft drinks vendor outside the gates of the Immigration department was running a form-filling service. Flipping open his laptop, my stall holder-cum-bureaucratic guardian angel, typed out my application, applied one of my photos (always take spares with you when travelling abroad) and printed it off within the space of three minutes flat.

He and his kind should have been running the Immigration service in the first place.

Back in the hangar and now learning fast the sharp elbowed routine of how to behave, I matriculated past desk one, settling down to observe my forms proceed from out-tray on desk two to in-tray on desk three and so on, with the gimlet-eyed concentration of a starving bird of prey. You had to sit and wait to be called forward to clarify minute points of detail, a severe test of anyone's patience. Progress was measured geologically.

When my forms got stuck in an in tray for twenty minutes or so, I would gently probe the call forward routine oozing humility from every pore, to ask politely if he (always he) could be so good as to apply the appropriate stamp and move the documents on. An all-important demeanour of humour with goodwill is essential for cooperation with any bureaucracy worldwide. Assertiveness almost never works.

The whole atmosphere and demeanour of the bureaucrats was affable and courteous, provided you stuck to the rules. It mattered little how long it would all take. A TV mounted in one corner of the hall broadcast a cricket match, giving the officials ample cause to admire the ground strokes or spin bowling of their favourite players. Luckily, the Delhi Daredevils were winning, keeping the officials in a good mood, while steam rose quietly from the long-suffering applicants. The tolerance of those for whom cricket remained a mystery was especially tested.

After seven hours, the process approached closing time for the day, after which we would be asked to return the next morning to start over. By then I had reached desk nineteen, and I was called forward to the penultimate clerk who signed my papers, throwing them with a flourish into the last in tray for InCharge to approve. Sitting on his raised pedestal above us lesser mortals, as undisputed arbiter of the final entry visa stamp, two of us were summoned before him simultaneously, the last supplicants of the day to undergo this final procedure. My fellow sufferer was a Four-ring Taiwanese airline pilot in full company uniform. InCharge flicked through his bright blue Chinese language passport and glared at me, exclaiming, "This isn't you!"

Until now, I had nursed the icy reptilian calm necessary for such occasions. But at this very last of seven hours of procedural bear traps, I nearly lost it. "No. That's him, he's the airline pilot!" I cried and pointed at the same time. Luckily, InCharge took my exclamation well, seeing the funny side rather than condemning me to return to desk one again. Two quick passport stamps and the pilot and I got out with a sense of blessed relief and a quick farewell to each other, before parting company for ever.

This story is not just a reminder to avoid Indian Immigration in future, but also because it says so much about context. The sense of helplessness in the face of seemingly mindless bureaucracy stays with me years later. But it was and remains, a neat metaphor for modern India – almost religious adherence to procedure regardless of the time it may take, but all done with goodwill and charm. Make sure you obey the rules though.

That day, I learned so much from observation of human nature under stress – saying I had enjoyed the experience, would be an exaggeration. But did I gain insights from it? Definitely. These started with realising that whatever the misfortune there are always others worse off than you. Context started to work on me providing the essential perspective to conclude – 'This was not all that serious, not so hugely time consuming, nobody died and what a story could later be told!'.

Fair exchange for finding literary material? Well maybe, but don't ask me to go through it again. I just keep repeating to myself – context is everything.

Can government connect with individuals?

My Indian experience resulted from petty crime, imposing on me bureaucracy and procedure at the most intricate personal scale. But what of large-scale social procedures and the governing of whole nations? Surely empathy is rare, indeed non-existent, at the collective level while pursuit of the greater good for most of the population is the more practical objective? Does empathy and sympathetic understanding of people as individuals have any part to play at a national scale of social process? Can any bureaucracy operate empathetically taking into consideration unique context as well as cultural and judicial procedure? Most would answer with an emphatic no. Government procedures have no capacity to apply such exalted levels of understanding of the human condition. Surely, not.

Empathy in governance? I think I know of one example, now lost to history and perhaps, inadequately documented, but an early illustration of state-sponsored deep understanding of people and communities who, despite diverse cultures have come to form a cultural, if not national, entity despite very diverse origins.

The birth and evolution of the state of Sarawak in northern Borneo, evolving nearly one hundred and fifty years ago and lasting until 1946, is my case in point. Now part of federal Malaysia, Sarawak is as different to the peninsula of West Malaysia and its states, dominated by Kuala Lumpur its federal capital, as say, northern Thailand is to Bangkok. The contrast of rural versus metropolitan values is as common to Malaysia as to anywhere in the world, but Sarawak is also a world away from many of the cultural and even racial tensions that exist on mainland Malaysia.

Sarawak evolved as almost the personal fiefdom of the Brooke family, who were granted vast areas of jungle by the British East India Company (BEIC) via obscure concessions dating from the eighteenth and nineteenth centuries. The indigenous population of Dayaks had a way of life initially little imposed upon in their jungle homes, by the arrival on their coast of a few Europeans and progressively, many more Chinese settlers. The Brookes, notionally backed by the BEIC in faraway Calcutta, were tolerated by the locals because they left them largely alone while providing an offshore defensive shield against marauding pirates usually from across the South China Sea. This prospect of protection, more than any recognised authority to be granting land rights, probably enabled much imperialist expansion worldwide, but it seemed to work benignly for Sarawak.

No doubt applying a large measure of self-appointed noblesse oblige, the Brookes family progressively granted part of the land to subsistence farmers and latterly the start of the palm oil plantation industry. The Dayaks would have suffered a loss of hunting terrain, but by the mid-nineteenth century, large numbers of them were leaving the forests to take advantage of better employment opportunities in small trading ports up and down the coast. The Brookes ruled as Rajahs, almost Indian style, from 1841 to as recently as 1946 when the British government, unpopularly for many, converted the country into a more conventional colonial status. It became part of federated Malaysia in 1963, again a decision that did not sit comfortably with all.

In 2012, I went to Kuching, Sarawak's capital, and onwards up the coast to review plans for a new city with the unprepossessing name of Mukah. My local hosts were fellow town planners, architects and engineers, a mix of both Malays and Hong Chinese, most of whom were descendants of immigrants to this east Malaysian state several generations previously. I delicately probed the apparently benign landlord-tenant relationship based on the Brookes as white Rajahs. I had read something of this history before arriving, with the Brookes effectively operating as self-appointed landlords, and local people as their tenants and rent payers. To what extent had the latter become subjects of the rajah-style landowner and did this stand up to post-colonial scrutiny?

To my surprise, the reputation of the Brooke family and the last Rajah - Charles Vyner deWindt Brooke - was stoutly defended by my hosts. His reputation and that of his family seemed to have been one of enlightened autocracy. This still baffles western Malays for whom experience of colonial history at the hands of less altruistic European rubber planters on the peninsula was quite different. Claims to property ownership were invariably contested more strongly in western Malaysia after a short run and unsuccessful communist insurgency during the 1950s, while the country was moving towards post-colonial independence.

Overall, Malaysia's population is dominated by western Malaysia on the peninsula, running down towards Singapore, so the received wisdom of the majority there is that Sarawak would have had similar colonial experience. It did not. In Sarawak, the Brookes were canny rulers, banning Christian missionaries and many other bearers of western culture from entering their fiefdom, while outlawing native head-hunting with punitive expeditions into the jungle interior to stop this practice.

They are recorded as managing the influx of immigrant, entrepreneurial Chinese in relation to local indigenous groups with a skill many would envy today. They seem to have been a throwback to a period pre-dating the mass colonial age, when genuine respect of local people including a deep cultural knowledge and awareness of their language and customs was expected of titular rulers, compensating for their own racial and religious differences with the indigenous population. Something similar may have existed in parts of India before the onset of large-scale European immigration after the Napoleonic Wars. But after the Army mutiny of 1857, for which the British Raj was largely responsible via a bovine ignorance of cultural sensitivities, any benign atmosphere between the rulers and the ruled started to evaporate.

In Sarawak, there were doubtless examples of Dayak communities being progressively removed from their traditional lands as the immigrant planters moved in, but at the same time, there will have been progressive absorption of the indigenes typical of so many other migrant movements worldwide. The point here is that Sarawak was ruled by a benign autocracy that may have deployed acute social awareness as its central tenet. Empathy is not sympathy or preference for one side over another. It would have needed a delicate balance in terms of judgement needed to dispense justice locally, particularly as these concerned land rights for settlement by the different communities.

The Chinese influx was coming anyway and unlikely to be prevented, from mainland China and other emigration routes from Singapore to the west and French Indo China to the north. But the Brookes respected Dayak culture as well, ruling out head hunting but also denying Christian missionary access to native peoples who might have regarded the principles of monotheistic theology alien to their animistic beliefs. These practices were most unusual as part of European colonial experience. Nuanced application of land rights and dispensation of justice that was largely devoid of racial bias relating to property and settlement, seems to have been part of the character of the Brooke family's ruler's mission, putting aside the rights or wrongs of how they got to be there in the first place.

No doubt for some, these will be deeply controversial arguments in an era when European colonialism is vilified as a universal social evil regardless of historical facts. But immigration and population flux by groups materially better or worse off than host populations, has been going on since humans emerged from their caves. And it is likely to continue, because social evolution is dynamic, and some communities thrive while others atrophy. Juxtaposing populations at different levels of development and thus material wealth is a constant refrain of history, sometimes with painful consequences. How different groups are governed, by whose rules, and with what degree of respect for the less well-off, whether hosts or incomers, all combine to determine whether such governance amounts to wrongdoing or something more empathetic. In the case of the Brooke family, the results in Sarawak probably owe more to social awareness – governance through imaginative identification with those governed - than in most cases elsewhere.

If you suspect my interpretation of this history to be overly partial, try an excellent book by Nicholas Monsarrat, *The White Rajah.*

Context is everything

It is a great test of anyone's objectivity to put aside current prejudices such as, 'all bureaucracy stifles progress', or 'colonialism is all bad' and look rationally at a case solely on its own merits. Context is everything. I look back on my experience with Indian Immigration with affection as well as dread because it taught me so much about human nature. I reflect now on a colonial experience already long past when I visited Sarawak, without the modern preconceptions of the whole process being bad. There is a strong case to be made that Sarawak has a happier colonial legacy than mainland Malaysia. How wonderful it would be to find an example of altruistic and empathetic government at the national level in our modern era! Is it still possible in our multi-cultural world?

Can I maintain my objectivity in the face of received wisdom or political correctness? Probably not, because there is usually insufficient time to set out the complete picture of why something is the way it is – or was. However, there is little doubt that to develop our understanding of other cultures or situations with which we are not already familiar, it is not sufficient merely to hear one or two witnesses and then make up our minds. An understanding of the history, politics and society of your own country should be sufficient to enable an understanding that you cannot lightly make up your mind about those of others. If you can, it is far better to absorb impressions first-hand because anything written or spoken is already someone else's own filter in operation. Making up one's own mind is difficult and demanding and requires the self-confidence not to jump to early conclusions or even to make judgements at all if the evidence seems incomplete.

If more of us could desist from applying cultural or national stereotypes to our judgements, it would make for a better and more tolerant world. Easily said; I am as guilty of forming stereotypes as the next man, and I need to learn that every person or circumstance is unique. "The way things are done around here," is a phrase hiding a lot of cultural depth. An historical equivalent might be, "The way things were," but the principle of needing to understand the big picture holds good. Interpreting historical facts truthfully is unlikely to be achieved by adopting the modern and sometimes self-righteous clothing of today's intellectual certainty. Finding a contextualised truth about anything or anybody is hard to do, and my next chapters look at how finding ways to get along with people and generating empathy can help.

Chapter 8

Learning from Cultural Diversity

How did I come to draw my conclusions about the fractures appearing in society? I describe my early years growing up, making the first of multiple journeys overseas and what they taught me about connecting with people from other cultures and building meaningful relationships.

*

I believe that not being noticed is the start of so many children's problems, leading either to further isolation or a more destructive demonstration of getting noticed all too clearly. In the latter case, antisocial acts kick off for little more than wanting to move swiftly from notice to notoriety. I sometimes think 'Notice me, notice me!' is the silent prayer of all kids feeling lost while growing up. If their friends and the grownups in their lives just responded positively to that, a lot of antisocial behaviour would never happen. 'You're dissing me!' might no longer represent local vernacular or the latest street talk, but the principle of what it means is timeless and without borders. Disrespect may be a noun turned verb, but it captures a fundamental human need. If everyone could be afforded a measure of respect after being noticed, the sense of inferiority engendered by its opposite would not lead to so many problems.

Anyone writing on a theme of human connectivity through building and maintaining human relationships ought, sooner or later, to set out their credentials to explain how they have arrived at their views. So, this chapter describes my navigating through childhood and early adulthood, slowly building social awareness to find connection with strangers - and sometimes not. We now call this seeking empathy, but I would not have called it that at the time and I have since acquired only a small number of the answers about how human relations work. My experience is no better than others, but it explains how I arrived at where I am. You, dear reader, will have just as effective experience as mine, provided you keep in mind the link to wider human relations. Context remains the key!

Part of the essence of empathy is its uniqueness. Everyone's journey of connection with their fellow man or woman will be individually defined, but they all contain a common strain of getting noticed and exchanging mutual respect. Zulus in southern Africa understand this right from when they meet. Their greeting to a stranger is 'Sawubona!', meaning, 'I see you!'. But this is more than simply seeing; it is a recognition that you matter to me because you are there before me and we have now met. The traditional reply is 'Shiboka!', meaning, 'I exist for you!'. Getting respect through being noticed and acknowledging it? Critically important.

Suggesting I know what works for others when making connections with people breaks a cardinal uniqueness rule of empathy, because it implies the application of my experience into that of others. Each encounter is unique, and context is everything. Nonetheless, we can learn from each other's experiences in many ways and I hope that you might learn something new and useful from mine. This chapter begins by recounting where my experiences started.

Perspectives on home and school
As I recounted in my chapter on the importance of place, I grew up on one of Britain's peripheral peninsulas, not quite remote in a Hebridean island sense, but a long way from anywhere with a big population. Pembrokeshire in the far west of Wales, is a

magical place surrounded by sea on three sides and subjected to most northern European influences from Welsh and Irish Celts, through Vikings, Normans, Flemish and latterly, English cultures, all of whom left their mark on settlements and place names. But the longest inhabitants of the place reveal themselves through the imagination - the bards, druids and sea faring traders who came before us. And only if you are very quiet, under the Maytime bluebells, the little people might reveal themselves as the true natives of this ancient place. They don't need to be noticed, but they like a bit of respect.

Idyllic in many ways, my home county was very much a place of dreams while growing up. But it also struggled to offer a sense of being at the centre of the universe – important for me seeking my small place in it. Urgency there was not. Mañana to a Pembrokeian is an expression of the immediate. "Good God, you want it that quickly? I wer' thinkin' Tuesday fortnite more like!"

My mum and dad must have reflected on this remoteness, by deciding to send me away to school. In mum's inimitable phrase, I would then be able, "To see over the garden wall," an objective which I have pursued ever since. In September 1959, approaching my ninth birthday, they put me on the Worcester train with instructions to get off at Colwall, underneath the Malvern Hills. The Downs School was then my destination each term for the next four and a half years; space and time to develop personality on my own terms, make friends with many - and avoid a few.

Thanks to careful parental selection, that school was a predominantly caring place, founded by Quakers and thus more *Swallows and Amazons* than *Tom Brown's Schooldays*. Thence, to Malvern over the Hills, for another four plus years, emerging semi-formed, but independent of spirit at eighteen, into my own dawn of adulthood.

Boarding schools have come in for much criticism in recent years, apart from the privilege they imply, because they extract children from the home environment to a place where parental influence is diminished, self-reliance is expected early on and expressions of love and affection are discouraged. But there is an instructive parallel between a boarding school and the internet that I challenged in my first chapter, the former representing a physical cockpit, the latter a psychological one. Both environments are goldfish bowls where everyone's swimming motion is permanently under the microscope of social comment often negatively, as that offers cheap fun to the observer and his audience. You can rarely hide in digital space, also true in a boarding school, separated physically from the filter of home and parental influence with the wise counsel they might offer.

Most pre-teens seemed to cope happily enough with the boarding experience, secure in the knowledge that parents were only a letter (compulsory on Sunday afternoons) or a weekend visit away. I saw a few examples of boys (sadly, no girls at my schools throughout the 1960s) who did not fit in. Such misfits usually displayed a lack of self-confidence in who and what they were, rather than the opposite and a consequent inability to cope with the harsher aspects of an institutional life. One or two of these lost souls were close friends, their otherness sometimes appealing. Fairly conventional myself, I was always curious about how others might see the world differently to the common herd. The herd thundered on regardless.

The worst manifestations of otherness were occasional needling or bating of those who seemed not to fit in. Open confrontation was rare, subtle wheedling to induce a temper tantrum much more common. Those who could not control their emotions lashed out verbally or physically. Usually the same culprits doing the bating and the same victims succumbing, it was seen as the best of spectator sports when someone lost control. We were fascinated by the destructive power of bad temper as chairs were thrown, classroom desks turned over, or beds upended in the dormitory.

Mental bullying was much more common than its physical alternative, and like all schools anywhere, learning to cope was vital. You are never alone in a bear pit. It is just a matter of finding your allies in joint defence against the grizzlies. And a lot of life is a bear pit, not just schools. We are a competitive species and while overt bullying is rare and can be called out, there are always people pushing you around before you gain their respect. Expectations that you can hold your own and contribute, while respecting that of others, is a delicate balance and critical to team building. Fitting into a team is what a lot of community life is all about, especially in a supercharged goldfish bowl like a boarding school. So, all too easily, the grizzlies in the bearpit are not just dysfunctional types you might encounter along the way, but your own inner drive to keep going, not let yourself down and hopefully, to excel at something, somewhere and somehow. Notice me, notice me! In seeking to get noticed, many of the demons are generated inside you, because self-respect is the start of gaining respect from others.

My childhood was, by and large, happy, and I know that there was a lot of good fortune in that. To be able to look forward positively, you need to be able to look back objectively and say, "This was good and that was not, but it was all experience!" After all, the space between past and future is but an instant, so the two are closely related when finding the way on life's journey. It is the one journey that never stops – from growing up to growing old, learning to get along with nearly everybody, content within your own skin while dodging the few psychopaths on the way. It is that journey in life that you travel maybe some of the way with others, but mostly on your own. You must make of it what you will. That is not depressing – being alone is very different from being lonely, and empathy with surroundings can be your close companion.

Over the garden wall – "Go West Young Man, Go West!"

The Preseli Mountains of north Pembrokeshire are the last point of Britain overflown by airplanes heading west for the US or Canada. From there, on a clear summer's evening, you can follow their jet trails when they reach cruising height out of Heathrow over the west of England, all the way to when they sink into the far west over the Atlantic with the setting sun - white when you first see them, pink, shading to a darker red as they disappear over the western edge of the world on a clear evening. They are probably visible for over three hundred miles or fully forty-five minutes at an airspeed of five hundred knots. They change direction over the navigation beacon at Strumble Head, west of Fishguard, so Pembrokeshire sets their course – a bigger navigational deal in the 1940s and 1950s than in 1969, but still a romantic indicator for my first long distance destination. How could I go anywhere else?

Aged eighteen, I walked those Preseli Hills, imagining the destinations of those airline passengers and wishing to be going there with them. Rural life was just too limiting for me; *Got to Get Away*, as in Georgie Fame's hit song that year. Hippie songs from Haight Ashbury's summer of love such as Bob Lind's *Bright Elusive Butterfly of Love,* beckoned me westwards, but also Glenn Campbell's *Wichita Line Man* to which I hummed myself to sleep that early summer of imminent liberation. After all, if spaced out hippies and buttoned-down telephone linesmen could both sing about finding love through a butterfly net or a phone wire, there must be something out there worth going to see. I just had to go empathize – American phrase, American spelling.

With my Visitors Visa casually ignored, (how times have changed) New York's state employment bureau still offered the best prospect of getting a job. I had done quite a bit of outdoor hiking and orienteering as part of the Duke of Edinburgh's Gold award back home, so I got hired by the Kiwanis Summer Camp Club in upstate Copake Falls, on the Massachusetts-New York state border - starting in three days' time! Marlon, the camp director, interviewing counsellor candidates in the Employment Bureau, explained that lots of the young campers would be wise-arse city types, but that never having seen woodland countryside before, they would go pretty wild in so much space. For all of their street wisdom, they were usually also pretty scared of the dark, in short supply in the then high-density tenements of Brooklyn, the Bronx and still, in those days, the lower east side of Manhattan, now much more an upmarket venue. He seemed to like me and my background, so I got hired to run the campouts in the woods. I would probably also be a quaint reminder to the kids that some people speak English "funny."

Most of the campers turned out to be no trouble at all and a joy to be with. "Hey Counsellor, I've found nature", was a constant cry as they brought you a new creepie-crawly to look at. But one or two, like everywhere, let down the rest. Otto was a real standout eleven-year-old troublemaker who showed every sign of not wanting to be there. While a born athlete, Otto was also an Olympic standard swearer, cussing everyone in the most colourful language and phrasing. "F... you, you're still in your mother's stomach," he would yell in a fit of quivering rage at the latest injustice. It was hard not to laugh, as he would then lash out with feet or fists.

It is clearly the right of shockers to shock and not be laughed at, as I quickly learned.

Some of the counsellors applied an old-fashioned routine of soap in the mouth, "To wash out your filthy language 'Atto!'" while others had him running around the bunkhouse thirty, forty, then fifty times, until late in the night. Otto would just never give up. He seemed to relish the challenge of facing us all down. Like so many troubled kids, it was probably quality attention that he really craved. If he had known the word, he would have said that no one was empathising with him. The street vocabulary of disrespect - "You are dissing me man!" was still a few years away.

But Otto was also very creative, and the other kids would follow his lead if he chose to take it. He was at his best in such circumstances. He composed a brilliant marching song for our Bunk Four campout, focused on rude observations about us counsellors, and the other boys would join in marching along the Appalachian Trail in the Catskill Mountains like a bunch of trainee marines. His disdain for authority extended to many of his fellow campers whom he regarded as toadies of the system. But Otto was also their star performer; his bunkhouse mates would sing his song all day. He was a pain to most of them, but he was their pain and no one else's. Teams have been built around less-promising relationships throughout history. I hope Otto found a career in music, show business or even ballet, as he was so athletic; he would have been a natural if he could only have found a way to channel life's frustrations positively. He just needed a bit of notice and respect.

Some of the girls were a different kind of challenge. At thirteen or fourteen, they were artfully capable of wind ups by developing real or faked crushes on male counsellors only a few years older than themselves. Nadia followed me everywhere for a few days, saying things like, "Lucky water!" when I was washing my face in a stream during a campout trek. She gave up on me pretty soon, and fixed her loving gaze on Ronnie Grunberg, the swimming counsellor, who, despite a thirty-cigarettes a day habit, could do three lengths of the pool under water. My "English ahhccent" could not compete with that. Maybe it was Ronnie's red, vintage, 1963 Mustang that Nadia really fancied.

1969 was the year that astronauts first landed on the moon watched by us campers and counsellors alike in grainy black and white late at night on the only TV. There were whoops and cheers as Neil Armstrong stepped off the moon lander with his immortal words about small steps by man and bigger ones for mankind. My fellow counsellors also included Barry Flast of New York rock group, *St Stephen,* who, through that early summer, helped generate the Woodstock pop festival outside the village of Bethel. The venue was only confirmed a week before the event and on our day off, we crossed the Hudson River in Ronnie's Mustang and tried, but failed, to get onto the festival site because of the endless traffic lines. So near, yet so far, but floating across the fields sitting on the car's open topped trunk lid, we still heard the distant strains of the *Star-Spangled Banner,* interpreted subversively by Jimi Hendrix. I counted myself as a Woodstock veteran after that.

After that, I travelled across Canada and the US by Greyhound, making it to my San Francisco west coast goal. But the Bay City had lost its summer of love atmosphere from only two years previously. Drug hangovers last longer than the alcoholic variety. Heading back through the Deep South, I met a very different 'Yew Ess of Aye' in the rural backwaters of Alabama, but even among people with a very different take on life - especially race - there was a welcome and an agreement to differ for a visitor passing through. Hospitality usually works worldwide if you also respect the hosts and agree to disagree.

Those early months after school, finding my way in another country, were a great introduction to the process of connecting with friends just through doing stuff together, building teams towards a common task. I had caught the travel bug.

Matemanship in Western Australia

At the end of my second University year in Oxford, I was ready to go journeying again, riding the wave of programmes that existed in the early seventies to encourage youngsters to travel. Jumping on a little-known award programme, promoted from Federal Australia to encourage graduates to go live there, I found myself a long summer vacation job working in the remote outback of north Western Australia (WA) on a water resources research project. Getting there was a mission and to a very different world when I arrived. Kids from deprived backgrounds around New York had been a first adult test of getting along with people. Hard-bitten drillers in a remote desert location was the next.

Three days driving the twelve hundred miles north from Perth in a Series Four Land Rover to the remote Pilbara region impressed on me the nature of remoteness. I went as co-driver to one of the WA's Department of Mines' geologists, Bob Leach – another Brit - to take over from Chief Geologist Angus Davidson, due to return after three months in the bush to Perth - to get married, no less. We were there to locate new water resources for the burgeoning iron ore industry expanding fast throughout the Pilbara, supplying mining townships and huge new ship handling facilities at Port Hedland, feeding the voracious appetite of Chinese and Japanese steel mills far away to the north. The terrain of our De Grey river research area was very dry with the aquifer groundwater found at depth, tens if not hundreds of metres below the surface.

Apart from the two geologists, the crew comprised some twelve drillers split into two teams with a tough and highly experienced foreman known to all as Boss John, a man who was not in the habit of taking prisoners. All had signed up for lengthy periods of remote living in caravans hundreds of miles from their homes. By any definition, this was a hardship location for uncompromising men who earned their living from tough physical work - a big contrast with young kids in an American summer camp. These drillers had been hardened by life experience; maybe the New York kids were just embarking on theirs?

I had guessed that such men were, in the main, pretty rough diamonds; I had not appreciated that most were also diamonds in the rough. Like seamen, they were a superstitious lot and would not share their caravan campsite living quarters with the geologists, whom they unceremoniously called Golliwogs. If this had been a racial slur instead of a play on words, it would have made no difference; these men spoke as they found, with no nuance of political correctness.

Angus lived in glorious isolation, using two caravans, one to sleep in, the other as a field office, about two miles from the drilling crews and nearby to one of the few patches of open water in the region. The drillers, meanwhile, had their own caravan park and would invite us over for beers and we would invite them back. But we never bunked or ate most meals together. This was a traditional – almost naval – arrangement but it seemed to work. Bob and I set up tents in Angus's camp, safe in the knowledge that in the July winter, the open water was not infested with mosquitoes. It was an idyllic spot just off the coastal highway, running away northwards hundreds of miles to Broome in the Kimberley region and eventually, Darwin.

Our daily routine was tough, mildly hazardous but repetitive, so every opportunity for diversions at someone's expense was seized gleefully. Men in the 1970s, especially those doing tough manual labour, were never tactile, but they replaced this mildly homophobic froideur, with constant humour that often got quite intimate. The ability to take part in, go along with or accept being the butt of the practical jokes was part of the bonding - or its opposite, the means of winkling out those who could not play by the rules. This may seem strange in an apparently more caring twenty-first century society where men are expected to show their emotions and even hug each other as part of more open expressive relationships.

But this remains surface behaviour and teams are still built from recognising the ability to cope with adversity, whether to go out of the cave to kill mammoths, fight wars shoulder-to-shoulder or merely work together in potentially hazardous circumstances based on mutual trust and reliance. The silly games may have been just that, but I suspect they had and still have, a deeper purpose. 'Will I be able to rely on this person in a crisis or not? Let me test the water and see!' was the unsaid thought.

In Australia, this tradition runs deep. The history of occupation of the vastness of the continent by so few Europeans (displacing more, but still not numerous indigenous groups) has built a huge belief in and respect for self-reliance. When there is no one else around, you fix the horse's hoof or the car's puncture, "On yer own, mite!" This is a big contrast with divisions of labour in socially stratified Europe, for whom the early white migrants to Australia engendered an abiding contempt. It also built the tradition of matemanship. There were so few others around in the vast Australian emptiness that you came to rely on each other like brothers, never ever to let each other down. Proving you were a mate was hard and testing, but once established, the bond was for life. Nothing so intense seems to exist in other cultures I have encountered, but when an outback Ozzie calls you mate, as more than just a passing remark, he usually means it and you better treat the moniker with respect. It is not easily won.

Under the last white rulers of South Africa and Rhodesia

There are regimes in the world that invite instant judgements not only about themselves but also those who choose to visit. Nowhere was this more true than South Africa during its apartheid years. The anti-apartheid movement was well organized and focused, in its implacable opposition to the white-ruled Republic. And with considerable justification. Quite apart from the denial of human rights and the cruelty with which it was implemented, it seemed like a social regime and experiment in urban and rural settlement patterns that could never work. Societies just don't work to such rigid rules.

But did this explain people's reluctance to have anything to do with the country and its people? Would it not be a good thing to go see and form one's own opinions rather than adopt the blanket disapproval so much the fashion among the student communities of which I was, by 1973, a four-year paid-up member?

Having defied the received wisdom of the time not to go there, my impressions of South Africa at the height of its apartheid era confirmed to me that this was a way of arranging things that could never work. I wrote my post graduate dissertation on the subject and it got commended, but I hope that was for content, not political correctness. What really struck home to me were some of the visceral experiences of watching minor struggles in action between a white-run government and a black majority populace.

I found a three-month long vacation job working for the Johannesburg City Council as a lowly, junior town planner in their Master Plan and Design Department. Fortunately, I was supernumerary to their mainstream functions, so free to fit in where they wanted me - a quiet advantage for work experience candidates that I recommend wherever students can find it. And there was so much to see, not all good, but all instructive when adopting an almost anthropological approach to the task.

We tend to associate apartheid with segregated buses, schools and park benches, but the principle of separate homelands and spatial settlement of people of different races was a far more profound aspect of the apartheid regime. In Jo'burg's City Planning Department, I would be close to the heart of its day-to-day management.

One of my early assignments was to accompany a senior planner on a site visit to Soweto, the enormous township for black workers twenty miles south west of the city. The government were looking for sites for new schools and the city planners were called in to assist. The local Non-European Affairs Department (NEAD) staffed by stalwarts of the apartheid philosophy, did not approve, voicing their views loudly that children had no place in a workers only dormitory community.

Soweto is now a thriving city, but in the early 1970s, it was bleak, a workers dormitory in every sense. When we reached a government stores office that might be suited for conversion to a school, we found there had been a break-in the night before and furniture and fittings had been smashed up. The diminutive five foot-tall official from NEAD who was escorting us went apoplectic and screamed about neglect of duty to the huge warrior-like security guard dressed in a ragged, blue uniform. The guard was a Zulu appointed to his post through the divide and rule principle in a mainly Xhosa part of the township. He bore this dressing down with silent dignity. His quiet demeanour enraged the official even more, so the shorter man grabbed the one unbroken chair to stand on, so he could reach the security guard's face to slap it.

I watched in horror, waiting for this little Hitler to be pile-driven into the floor in retaliation, but it never happened. This was a perfect metaphor for the relationship between races at the time. A minority expecting perfect obedience and compliance to white mans' rules, and a black majority bearing it - on this occasion, at least – with massive forbearance and dignity. On return to Jo'burg, we planners filed a complaint against the NEAD official, but I doubt anything will have happened. I wonder where both the protagonists are now and what they would have to say to each other. So much has changed and South Africa has been a miracle of forgiveness.

I was given lots of time off, so decided to hitchhike for a few days to Salisbury (now Harare) in the then war-torn Rhodesia, to the north. The journey through the northern Transvaal was far from easy with only short rides, including one from a bible-bashing Afrikaner who politely, but firmly, got me reading Exodus to his kids so they could hear English spoken 'korrectlee' as he put it. I thought it best to ask to be dropped in the next town and could see that with more than eight hours to go to Salisbury, this might be a slow trip. While drinking a coke in a roadhouse outside Potgietersrus, a military looking type with a buzz cut approached me and offered a lift all the way. Good fortune - or too good to be true?

Dirk, I forget his second name nearly fifty years on, said he was a South African volunteer in the Rhodesian Light Infantry (RLI) engaged at that time in a vicious war with the Terrs, as they were known locally. These disparate groups were otherwise known (depending on your politics), as the African freedom fighters all around Rhodesia, to where they could infiltrate from neighbouring countries such as Zambia or Mozambique. Dirk was returning from leave and seemed to be well paid, driving a brand-new Ford Corsair, a model that had recently won the Paris Dakar Rally. He did not offer to open the boot, so I threw my bag on the back seat and we set off for Salisbury. Plenty of time to get perspective on an unfamiliar subject - bush warfare.

At Beit Bridge, the South Africa-Rhodesia border crossing, Dirk left me at Immigration, referring vaguely to paperwork to be dealt with elsewhere. Reunited after half an hour, we crossed the bridge into Matabeleland over Kipling's 'great, green, greasy' Limpopo River. I could see hippos basking up stream of the bridge. This seemed like heading into the real Africa, or at least, a white man's version of it.

Dirk had little time for us Brits and the soft European attitude to African independence movements, declaring his trust in the Ian Smith government to win the war. He delighted in telling me how a bush war was fought. The troops had discarded their normal automatic weapons and equipped themselves with sawn off shotguns, as close encounters with the enemy in thick bush were short and deadly. The first side to get off a blast of lead shot in a wide arc would win the battle. Grenades and mortars followed but scariest of all, were the machetes, used in hand-to-hand fighting to finish off those previously wounded by gunshot or explosives. No prisoners were taken.

On reaching the capital, I stayed a few days in Salisbury where there seemed to be no overt apartheid in action. Lots of the city bars were full of soldiers, black and white together, with young black girls circulating among them, innocently or with more mercenary intent. A day or two later and quite unexpectedly, I received a telephone message from Dirk offering me a return trip to Jo'burg the next day. I had only come to see the place and needed to get back to work, so I accepted. More good fortune or something else?

Once again, the boot of his powerful car remained firmly closed, so my bag stayed on the back seat for the long ride south. I started wondering about the curiosities around such a fortunate encounter. Twice in three days, Dirk had approached me out of the blue, admitted he was a South African mercenary in the Rhodesian army, kept me from a sight of the contents of the car boot, separated me from himself and his car at the Beit Bridge border and now only two days after 'returning from leave', he was heading back to South Africa again. What was going on? Weapons smuggling, maybe?

It would have been uncomfortable asking awkward questions. I remembered my professor at university who had advised me to keep my counsel when dealing with difficult situations. If he was half the soldier he claimed to be, leading a platoon of blood-thirsty bush troopers, Dirk would not have hesitated to get rid of me if he felt his cover was blown. I was not sorry to part company with him on arriving back a day later in Jo'burg's northern suburbs. But the lifts were welcome.

A few years later, when Rhodesia finally became Zimbabwe, stories about how the regime had been supported started appearing in the press. Weapons smuggling was the hottest of topics. Had I been the innocent cover for a profitable and even government-sponsored side-line? I will never know, but not asking questions, I survived to tell the tale.

There is probably no team building more important than when armed forces go to war. Unlike my father and his before him, I have no experience of war and what it does to men, and now women, under combat stress. But where experience ceases, imagination sometimes takes over, and I have always believed good team morale would be a matter of life or death in a war zone. To me, Dirk's sense of what he was fighting for was warped – by profit, if not ideology and probably both. But he may have understood teamwork better than me. A sense of belonging, even across a black-white divide may have evolved within his platoon, based solely on the survival imperative. Little wonder he held people with no such experience in contempt. My politics were probably less offensive than my naivete.

Many of the characteristics which made Angus Davidson's and Boss John's drilling teams in north west Australia an effective working unit would also have held good for a combat platoon in war. The puerile behaviour always had a purpose. I recall my dad recounting similar experience from war-torn North Africa and Italy from 1942 to 1945. Can I trust this person to be there for me if things go wrong? I will test his tolerance of some psychological stress now to find out. Of course, where this spills over into bullying, it becomes something else. We have seen several examples in recent years where army training failed to sustain the delicate balance between building morale through self and by extension, communal reliance and open intimidation that leads to cruelty for its own sake.

But challenging people to step up in stressful circumstances remains an essential part of growing up. Self-reliance is only built around an ability to cope and developing trust to form part of a team is only ever based on what your fellow team members feel about you. So back to Otto, our standout summer camp rebel from 1969. He knew instinctively the power of a good song to bind together his team of infantry, as they fondly imagined themselves to be, hiking the Appalachian Trail, as if it were a war zone. The imaginations of those boys needed little motivation, as they sought their future manhood through the power of group belonging. Their musical composer knew how best to capture it.

Out of the Anglophone bubble

Language is one of the cement blocks of culture and I was determined after qualifying academically, to break away from the anglophone comfort bubble that first travels had offered. I was still hearing my mum whispering in my ear, "Get over the garden wall." Between the mid-seventies and eighties, projects in Algeria, Morocco and Bolivia gave me the opportunities.

Algeria 1975 to 1982 – A valuable lesson in cultural perspective

On graduating in 1974, I joined an international planning and design consultancy and soon got myself assigned to a joint venture team from France and the UK, assembled near Annaba on Algeria's north east coast, providing technical advice to the national Algerian Steel Authority client – SoNaSid. Their main project was a huge, new, integrated steelworks, but a small group of us went there to examine prospects for a new town at Sidi Ammar on the hills to the west of the industrial complex. No one, least of all the government client, had yet thought that the steel workers would need accommodation, so we were a bit of a distraction to those fixated only on getting Algeria self-sufficient in steel making. Silo thinking on big picture issues such as this, is sadly a characteristic of some of the largest projects worldwide.

Typical new town planning in Algeria at the time centred around soulless, four storey walk-up apartments imported from their new international solidarity partners in the Soviet Union and East Germany. Post-colonial Algeria was gradually herding its people in one of two directions, a de-humanized socialist modernity for which the four storey concrete blocks were the perfect metaphor, or a steadily more conformist perception of a pre-colonial past with increasingly religious overtones. This was to cause trouble decades later, as I recorded in my chapter on trauma.

An urban master plan was called for and I managed to persuade the authorities that we planners needed to understand the true culture of the country, from which to recommend appropriate social and architectural forms for the new town. To my surprise, they agreed, and I was allowed to travel around the country absorbing flavours of Algerian urbanism, little understood or used, for over a century of colonialism and its more recent socialist opposite – imported cultures both. This meant heading south, away from the coast across the steep Atlas and Aurès mountain chains and into the Sahara. We would never have seriously considered recommending desert architecture in a coastal context, but who could come to Algeria and not see the real desert?

I was only allowed to go south if accompanied by an experienced local driver. Routes were poorly signposted and the desert beyond the Atlas Mountains was not somewhere to break down alone. I was introduced to Hamed, a young taxi driver recently recruited to the SoNaSid Administration. He jumped at the chance to revert to his former profession for the twelve-hundred-kilometre round trip south, proudly showing off his country to 'un Anglais'. Very early one morning, we set off in an ageing company issue Renault 4, on a round trip through Constantine, Batna, and Biskra, then past the ancient Roman ruins of Timgad, before entering the Sahara proper, with the ultimate oasis destinations of El Oued and Touggourt.

Long road trips are one of the best ways to get to know people, as I had found for better in Australia and worse in Rhodesia. Now, at the other end of the African continent, Algeria gave me a heaven-sent and very different opportunity to repeat the experience.

That trip also did wonders for my French, which Hamed, like all young men of his generation, spoke well, as well as to my understanding of a country whose tragic history had not ceased after nearly six decades of post-colonial rule. The journey took us through the Gorge du Roufi where the active rebellion against France had started in 1954. Little fortified towers in line of sight through the thirty-kilometre-long valley were still there in testament to the French military occupation from long ago. But more tragic were the old colonial farmsteads, covered in luxuriant purple bougainvillea but ruined and abandoned by their white settlers. They were deemed to be 'haram' (forbidden) for re-occupation by local people via both Muslim dialectic and socialist decree. So, they stood as silent sentinels to a lifestyle now abandoned.

Hamed was matter of fact about this recent history, giving me his, or perhaps his parents, carefully objective impressions of the war of independence, while he had still been very young. Later, I learned of the deep split between the freedom fighters (the FLN) and those who had been called up to fight for France, known since by all Algerians and those in the know in France as 'harkis'. From that civics lesson in school long ago, aged twelve, I knew a little of this history, but nothing compared with hearing it almost first-hand from a man who had grown up with it

What ironies the end of colonialism had generated ahead of independence. In fact, Algeria had merely swapped one set of cultural dependencies – colonial France - with another, so called international socialism. I noticed this in my own nuanced impressions, finding it easier to refer to France's involvement in Algeria as occupation, while seeing British intervention in Rhodesia two years before as merely un-enlightened colonialism. Where you come from defines much of what and how you perceive things.

The scenery got more and more spectacular as we drove south. The towns and villages seemed desperately poor, often with little visible economic activity. Occasional flashes of bright flowering shrubs along the road signified a ruined ex-French farmstead with wild purple bougainvillea left to grow uninterrupted for years since the places had become deserted. We drove up to one that had evidence of blast damage to one of its outer walls and Arabic graffiti warning the locals to stay away.

We travelled far through the desert on that trip to El Oued and Touggourt, deep into the Sahara, so very different to the north coast where we would be building our new town. But this exercise in perspective, both learning recent history and understanding the social hinterland for Algeria's rapid industrialisation, was essential for my better understanding of what and for whom, we would be planning. Empathy is not only born from meeting and relating to people, but to understand at least, some of the physical and historic context of their lives and circumstances. What modern film makers now call the backstory.

Little vignettes on that long trip struck me then and stay with me now. Leaving the oasis town of Touggourt on our return day, I noticed a strange single storey building on the edge of the oasis town, decked with colourful flags and streamers, very unlike the austere Algeria that I was now used to. Even more bizarre, there were a few girls dressed in bright veils and long flowing djellabas sitting outside. I asked Hamed who they were, and he was at first embarrassed, but slowly becoming more matter of fact. "C'est une bordelle," he said finally, "pour les filles tombées." Such a Victorian phrase; how had these girls become fallen?

He described the doleful pattern of failed marriages with husbands rejecting young wives before emigrating to the big cities or abroad. The girls' families sometimes offered no protection after such social disgrace, so the only safe place for them was the local shelter, as they called it, funded informally by prostitution services to be offered in return. He also admitted that girls could be expelled from their families for the apparently minor departure from strict social codes – merely talking to boys in the street. With the nearby gas fields of Hassi Messaoud, there was plenty of male demand for such services, but a further tragic twist was that family members would also feel themselves free to use the bordello's services. Filles tombées indeed.

This feature of a male-dominated culture, untouched in remote districts by Algeria's socialist revolution, made me ponder how far things had to evolve, before any true sense of liberation arrived for women and girls who fell victim to strict social traditions. I watched in the car mirror as a girl who must have been no more than twelve, stared after us, thinking how far removed her future life would be from my sister, or daughters of my own, yet unborn.

En route home, it was gathering dusk as we approached the lights of Constantine in the distance, Algeria's third largest city, perched high on a hill overlooking its deep gorge. Suddenly, a tiny gazelle, blinded by our headlights, froze in the middle of the road. Hamed braked and swerved, but we hit it a glancing blow as it tried to leap away. Hamed was touchingly upset, given his previous matter-of-fact attitude to human tragedy. We put the gazelle in the boot to carry home, with no real idea of what else to do. Leaving it for the birds to peck to death seemed worse. After a few kilometres, there was a banging and scraping from the back of the car. The animal had clearly only been stunned and wounded. Now suddenly awake, it was trying to escape.

Hamed was in a quandary about what to do, concerned that the police might take a dim view of exporting a wild animal from the desert. We stopped in the next village for him to phone his relations in Constantine, and he came back beaming with relief. We could take the gazelle to his Uncle Mahmoud's house where his family of four small children would look after it, or maybe eat it, I thought ruefully, as I could not see it surviving a broken leg. I kept that to myself.

Just so, did I get my first glimpse of Algerian family life in the rare circumstance of not being the main subject of interest for the assembled children as a foreign visitor. Of course, we had to stay for a meal, as it was by now getting dark and the roads were busy with late afternoon traffic. The four children clustered around the little gazelle, for whom a cardboard box had been found, lined with straw by the youngest child. They gazed in wonder at this little wild creature staring back at them with beautiful, frightened eyes, then at me, the foreign co-bearer of this magical gift from their Uncle Hamed.

We eventually sat down to an enormous meal of mechoui and rice – the delicious lamb kofta of the Atlas Mountains. Wine was brought out for the honoured western guest – Cuvée du Président – Algeria's finest, but no one else drank it. What is the polite response? To do justice to their hospitality, or respect their Muslim teetotalism? No right answer, so I self-consciously took a few sips and pushed the rest aside. By the time we were finished, Hamed and I were in no mood to hit the road again that evening for the one-hundred-and-fifty-kilometre final leg to Annaba on mountain roads. Uncle Mahmoud insisted we stay the night and, as the honoured guest, the children were turfed-out from their bedroom and I got to sleep in a double bed alone. My embarrassment soon gave way to dreamless sleep.

The next morning after a brief coffee and among fond farewells for a good journey, we left Constantine for Annaba. The gazelle had survived the night and was being fed milk by the youngest children, but I doubt it will have survived long and perhaps graced a fine mechoui at some later date, suitably disguised so the children would know nothing of what they had eaten.

I spent much time back and forth to Algeria up to the mid-1980s on new infrastructure projects, but life for foreign visitors and businesspeople got more and more insecure as the civil war of the 1990s loomed closer. Only rarely, were there further opportunities to witness close family life. I found it a bewitchingly beautiful place despite its sad and brutal recent history. Very much excluded from the modern tourist itineraries, Algeria remains broadly unknown to western visitors. It is, therefore, widely misunderstood but like everywhere in the world, the public and private faces of the place are very different, if you are ever lucky enough to get to see both.

Morocco 1977 – Don't buy a dog if you want to bark yourself

A similar assignment to plan a new town in neighbouring Morocco around the late 1970s provided less happy memories. Not because Morocco is unwelcoming; on the contrary, it has opened itself to the world far more than its large neighbour to the east following a wholly more benign end-of-colonial experience. The negative memories were entirely home grown within the leadership of our project team.

A multi-discipline assembly of British engineers, economists and planners was mustered in Rabat to write a pre-feasibility report for the World Bank on a new industrial and residential complex at Nador, four-hundred-kilometres away on the north coast of the Mediterranean. However, the team dynamics, so important to harmonious working, were almost destroyed by our director, who wanted to dictate how every aspect of the intended multilateral viability report would be written. The subjects covered specialties well beyond his own, including economics of raw material supply and demand, supply and transport of finished product to markets, likely growth of construction and operational staff and their accommodation needs, design schedules, precise site selection and associated infrastructure, environmental impacts and so on. Complex issues and well beyond the expertise of any one discipline. Arguably, this agenda was far too diverse a set of topics to put into one report, but the client (SNS, to differentiate itself from the agency with a similar task in neighbouring Algeria) was adamant that overseas aid agencies such as the World Bank who might be funding the project, were demanding one assessment of the whole task between two covers.

The director accompanied our diverse team of twelve different professionals to an upscale hotel in Rabat, where we were to be housed for as long as it would take to write our various analyses. He would transit back and forth to relevant ministries (wearing his three-piece grey suit, regardless of the August heat) to handle almost all third-party consultations by himself. With a singular absence of French or Arabic, he relied on an interpreter to receive on course briefings, assuring his, as opposed to our, client of progress back at our hotel, where he would return to brief us on new interpretations of the brief needed in our write-ups. Aside from our frustration at such limited direct access to relevant authorities, some of us felt that a site visit would be essential, arguing that site selection and impacts could not be conducted remotely. Despite his opposition, we did manage a three-day visit to the site, but reporting on that was discouraged, on the fatuous grounds that the report was supposed to confine itself to principles, not practice.

Steadily, the director imposed his will on the format and content of each chapter as if he was the ultimate author – which is the way it turned out, because our draft texts were all extensively cut down and edited before acceptance for publication. A lot of the critical recommendations that we felt were necessary were edited to draw a more positive conclusion about problems being solvable and timescales for design and construction being easily achievable.

The director's will prevailed over ours, as specialists, because of the differences in age, experience and seniority between us and the project manager and director himself. I think the project manager sympathised with our concerns, but he was not prepared to stand up to higher in-house authority. For some of us, this had been a first, or at least early, big career break – in my case, to be the representative of all urban master planning matters concerned with a workforce of thousands and their family dependants. How best to provide housing and community facilities for them was a big responsibility that I felt keenly but was barely allowed to express with any local sensitivity to the real issues.

The resulting report – luckily for me, extending well beyond the urban planning aspects – was an abject failure, and the big funding banks panned the recommendations, sending our ministry clients, and us, their consultants, back to the drawing board. There was a strong feeling among the team, who otherwise enjoyed what little time they could carve out as their own in Morocco, that we were badly led through an impossible brief. The dynamics of the team – its morale and self-belief – remained reasonably intact while on assignment in a hot August and September. Those two months coincided with Ramadan that year, which did not help our morale, with a complete absence of daytime refreshments throughout the hotel.

But when we got home to England, with the first reactions of the funding agencies and client started to emerge, the proverbial hit the fan. The director did not work again on technical assignments, only on corporate finance, where his skills seemed no more effective. He left the firm soon after.

Could its leadership have made this prestigious international assignment more effective? Undoubtedly, but I suspect that the project brief was wrongly cast in the first place. Too diverse a range of subjects for one report, remoteness from many of the issues needing to be understood and defined properly, but chiefly, not enough time to do the job thoroughly. Perhaps even the World Bank was also wrong asking for a single report across so many diverse subjects, trying to summarise the feasibility of a project that required so much more analysis than we were permitted to give.

The vital ingredient about individual and group motivation – a young team given its first exposure to a high-profile task with a lot hanging on it for client and consultants' credibility - served us well to get through the ordeal. We were thereby vaccinated against fear of failure in future planning projects by a valuable object lesson. When you have selected your team, let them do their work, otherwise portrayed in our office vernacular as, "If you want to bark yourself, don't buy a dog!"

Bolivia 1978-79 - A sense of resigned wellbeing

Another assignment just a year later saw me going to Bolivia for twelve months, this time accompanied by my new wife Sylvie, to participate in the planning and design of a new town and industrial complex. The overall purpose was to enable Bolivia to become a manufacturer – or at least assembler - of road vehicles. Like our Moroccan project, the Bolivian government client wanted a master plan with which to seek wider World Bank funding. This time, the job was not rushed or under resourced. These were the late and free spending 1970s, when World Bank money seemed to be easily available to industrialisation projects.

We formed up in a by-now familiar joint venture arrangement of Bolivian civil engineers and British planners. We blended well together from the start, despite a paucity of each other's mother tongues. Everyone was keen to participate in Bolivia's bold march towards an industrial future. Never underestimate the value of a worthy cause.

Site visits (no Morocco-style restrictions here) became day-long affairs by four-wheel drive vehicles with plenty of food and water taken along in case of breakdown in the arid and sparsely populated altiplano landscape. Breakdown rescue was not on the agenda and mobile phones were still military items the size of bricks wired to an even bigger battery. We did not have any.

There is a happy-go-lucky philosophy of the poorest people in Latin America, based on acceptance that they could influence little in their lives and improve their welfare almost not at all. Successive governments were renowned for attending to the needs of the campesinos long after they looked after themselves, so no one was holding their breath for change. The local villagers of Santivañez watched us come and go on our site visits with detached amusement, suspecting that little would change. A sense of resigned wellbeing gradually affected us all as sketches became drawings and then became three-dimensional designs, all drafted manually in the last days before computer-aided design.

The key ingredients of this were a project direction and management regime that allowed reasonable free rein to each professional group to generate their best proposals in the circumstances. In terms of long-term achievement, we concluded that we could do little to influence the actual implementation of our plans beyond some practical cost minimisation measures, so we ceased to worry whether we were going to change history or geography.

Little did we know that Bolivian government negotiations with Renault in Brazil and Mercedes Benz in Argentina were not going well and that maybe no vehicle parts would be arriving to fill the new assembly plants we were planning on site. I think a few crated vehicles were eventually shipped to Bolivia for disassembly before being put back together as wholly manufactured, supposedly Bolivian products. They were centre stage in a great fanfare of celebration a few years later but otherwise, little changed. Our work on paper finished in mid-1979 and we returned to the UK the slow way, via Lake Titicaca, Cuzco and eventually, Mexico. Happy carefree days.

Looking now at Google Earth more than four decades later, there are far fewer buildings on site than those we had planned, and little sign of vehicle assembly beyond lots of storage. But what a wonderful lark in Latin America for a year. That was the way things were in international development projects of the late 1970s; free spending plans some amounting to little more than pipedreams

Understanding team dynamics
These last three country examples from Algeria, Morocco and Bolivia, following more familiar but still new and challenging circumstances to start with, in the US, Australia and Southern Africa, served to teach me two principles about team building, leadership and the empathy needed to glue them together. The first is that to understand a place and its people properly, you aim to connect in equal measure, with communities as well as individuals. The task of gaining a sense of connection with people, and to become friends with other members of a team, may be more challenging in cultures contrasting widely with your own. But the rewards for doing so are, therefore, greater when achieved. Getting over that garden wall and finding exotic contrasts on the other side can be rewarding. Finding out that the exotic contrasts evolve into joint endeavour and common ground is more intoxicating still.

Such connections should never be confused with understanding group dynamics within a common language or culture. Individuals are as distinct from groups as those groups are distinct from others of contrasting cultures. There is no pigeon-holing to be done, despite our universal inclination to do so. Everyone is an individual and they will find their own place in a group without the need of a shoehorn.

A second principle learned from these project-based encounters pointed me to the essential elements of team morale. Long drawn-out training and eagerly sought experience with which young people in any profession or technical trade start such projects, will usually ensure they are already highly self-motivated to do a good job. They require little more management-speak encouragement from their bosses. Drive to apply oneself over long hours, night and day, is almost never an issue. The spur is not to let yourself or your team mates down. When presented with a significant contribution to a major project, most people want to work their socks off.

You can de-motivate people far more easily by interfering in their invariably positive intent to do the right thing. As I moved from project planner to management and eventually, the direction of such projects, I did my best to avoid excessive interference with competent people when they were getting on with their work. If you pick the right team to start with, let them find their way through team bonding processes for themselves and only get involved when things are visibly going wrong.

Leadership is only learned first-hand and face-to-face. Observing the body language, eye contact, tone and timbre of a good leader is critical in breeding the next generation of people training to do the same. I vividly remember watching and learning from good leadership in action. It almost never needs to raise its voice; it listens more than it speaks, it invariably sets an example through doing things right in preference to talking about them. And responding to good leadership is both uplifting to individual and team morale, but also motivational to the good leader him or herself to continue to do right by everyone. It is a benign cycle, needs savouring when you sense its presence and can never be taken for granted.

Following the principle that I espoused previously, observing an absence of effective leadership is just as instructive. Seeing poor leaders in action, whether through poor judgement about individual behaviour or the team's dynamics, broadcasting personal virtue as an experienced practitioner and a multitude of other sins that we all recognise when we see them, gives you clues as a young team member how not to treat people when promoted to the same position yourself.

None of this is available via the Internet, nor filtered through a flickering digital device screen. Leadership, both good and bad, has the most profound effect on either good or bad outcomes of any endeavour and it cannot be taught only by book learning or digital communication.

Just so, did I, like so many of my fellow planning, architectural and engineering contemporaries, slowly learn about empathy and its outcome of meaningful connections – the imaginative identification with others. This does not need the pre-requisite of liking everyone, though finding ways to get along with nearly everyone is a useful start. Rather, what is important is knowing that team players will be dependable in difficult and occasionally life-threatening circumstances. Give people the rope. They will usually not hang themselves.

I believe that such experience is simply not available when distilled through communications technology. You cannot either understand individuals and teams with whom you work, or the people you are seeking to serve, without face-to-face and more important mind-to-mind contact. Tempting though it will be in a pandemic world of the future to conduct such daily intercourse online, projects conducted remotely should always allow time and space for human contact. Overcoming social distance is not deliverable via hand-held telephones!

Chapter 9

Meeting People Halfway

Having written about the fracturing of society and my personal experience of triggering and developing meaningful connections with people, this chapter deals with how to cope with first encounters – of people, places and new cultures. This experience has served me well, so I hope it might help others when on their own journeys, or just living their lives in general.

*

You could look at this chapter as something of a travel guide, but I prefer the title 'encounter' guide. It is all about impressions made – both on you and then about you, as you encounter new experiences. It does not matter whether that means creating new impressions about new acquaintances, or from them, or gaining new impressions from new places locally or in a foreign land; you are still stimulating impressions. You can choose whether to 'swing by' as per the deliberately casual modern phrase, or to make and experience deeper impacts. I prefer the latter wherever there is time and space to do so.

This process of making an impression also needs some picking apart. You can see it as making sure you impress people – with charm, wisdom, eloquence, enthusiasm, strength of conviction, or whatever. But the most profound impressions start in the opposite direction - impressions on yourself. In other words, allowing a person, place or situation to impress themselves on you before returning the complement. That is one essence of the empathy behind meaningful connections, ensuring that they are two way. Merely meeting someone or going somewhere to broadcast your contribution to the world without listening to and sensing what you experience, will generate mixed reactions, at best. Allowing circumstances to seep into your own being first, before allowing the process to reverse direction, should allow the two-way process to last longer and go deeper.

In the days of the Grand Tour, gentlemen of means, and I am glad to say a fair few fortunate ladies, would have devoted a year or so to their education by visiting Italy and Greece, and for the more adventurous, Turkey or Syria, to bone up on their classical education. They would probably learn some of the languages and bring back a few artefacts, an Elgin Marble or two perhaps. On returning home, their adventures and the reflected glory of daring escapades would liven the conversation in the country house, London club or the Royal Geographical Society. Their general air of broad-minded education would probably attract admirers and improve marriage prospects. Making impressions indeed.

The difference between those travels for a privileged few and the mass tourism of today is not just numbers, but also the time taken. In our time-strapped world, the two or three-week holiday is all most of us wage-dependent slaves can manage. To cover any significant ground in that time requires military-style planning and a schedule to match. When I was small, my dad would introduce each new sight to behold as 'Roberts' Lightning Tours' – thirty minutes for Milan Cathedral or one hour maximum for Madurodam Model City in the Netherlands. We laughed at the superficiality of it but got around a lot.

During the average sun-soaked visit to the Mediterranean for northern Europeans or the Caribbean for Americans, the formula for most visitors has shifted over fifty years to lying on a pool-side sun lounger or on the beach, with little time for sight-seeing. Neither activity gives much opportunity to meet and converse with the locals. Little wonder they are called package holidays; the package remains tightly wrapped and returns home largely unopened.

Students on a gap year have a lot more time, enabling them, as some describe it, "To go round the world," although their grand tour conversazione when they return, always seems a bit limited. There is often too much reliance on itineraries that include such more or less Anglophonic stepping-stones as Dubai, Singapore, Australia, the US, then home. Acquaintances met on the way are often likely to have been fellow students on a similar quest, with the distinct possibility that if they remembered the encounters, rather like our 1960s, they were probably making it up. There is no doubt that gap year travels are hugely rewarding to those that do them, especially if they are linked with work experience in a different context to home life.

Recruiters that I know, and my own interview technique over many years, bear witness to wanting details of such travels from young graduate job candidates. At least as much time was spent discussing this travel experience as on the verification of academic qualifications. And rightly so. How else to find out what a candidate is really like, and how might they fit in to a team? For me, it was a danger sign if there was too much tendency to stick within the comfort zone of familiarity and little evidence of meeting the locals, however challenging that might have been. Curiosity is critical to an active intelligence, not served by languishing in comfort zones.

Business trips are (might that soon be 'were'?) similarly, a challenge to absorbing local culture. More so than for tourists, time is of the essence, even after the trip has been sanctioned by the bean counters. With so much sophisticated digital communication available today and the carbon footprint to consider, the era of the FIFO (Fly-In, Fly-Out) may now be a thing of the past. I well remember the worst of these typical schedules. They would include an overnight seven to ten-hour flight, a red-eyed, all-day meeting, struggling to stay awake through an evening meal with clients somewhere thoroughly forgettable in town together with more drinks than wisdom dictates, a few hours' sleep in an anonymous hotel room strangely similar to the one slept in on the other side of the world two weeks previously, and back home on the plane on the third day. Scope for meeting people, apart from other fellow sufferers? Zero. Absorption of local culture apart from the drive to and from the airport? Similarly, nugatory.

So, when, and if, the time and opportunity present themselves to really meet people away from home and try to get to know them, how is this best done? Time was the critical word in that question. Very little can be done without time on your side, but a little advance planning can help in the quest to find meaningful connections with strangers.

Here are a few ideas.

Travel alone

My first big overseas trips as the previous chapter explained, were mostly as a student when unattached romantically and thus, free to go my own way. I covered a lot of ground through the early seventies and over summer vacations – to the US and Canada, Australia, South Africa and Rhodesia in different years. But these were the classic Anglo-phonic stepping-stones, persuading me that I had to escape that comfort zone and seek work and travels in non-English speaking countries. From the late 1970s onwards, I have variously worked, lived in, and latterly just visited, over sixty of the world's one hundred and ninety-five countries. That is still less than a third of them, so there is a way to go.

Travelling or meeting people alone means not taking a double dose – your companion's and your own – of familiar comparisons with you as you journey about. I tried hard to adopt a mindset to avoid making invidious comparisons with the familiar, either positive or negative. But merely to experience differences without judgement is hard because perspective is essential as part of new experience. Many that you meet more readily when alone will press for information about where you come from. That question invites the start of the comparison conversation. With a little effort, it can remain fun and harmless. But it becomes negative the more one relates back to one's previous comfort zone.

It is more the conversation inside one's own head that is important. Do I see this new person or place in perspective to myself or own home, or am I seeing them just as they are? An absence of merit or de-merit points from personal judgement faculties makes sense but it takes an active effort of will and a clearing of the subconscious proclivity to compare. I am not sure I have ever fully achieved this state of neutral grace, but it is undoubtedly an aspiration for the open-minded traveller through time or space. See people and places for what they are rather than through the prism of comparison with the familiar.

Since getting married in 1977, the principle of travelling alone has obviously been less appealing. Almost all my travels for pleasure and a few for work are now accompanied with my partner in life. But in Sylvie, I inherited an unexpected bonus. She was born and brought up near Barcelona, but with a French father and taking her nationality from him, she was a foreigner in her birthplace and home country. This otherness can be an advantage in not seeing things always as the locals do. Culture shock for her was already made less impactful by her expatriate upbringing and latterly, via a large dose of love for the Britain she knew then and experienced for most of the subsequent decades. So, her frame of reference for subsequent travels has been different to mine, lacking the temptation that I now recognise, as often more British than French or Spanish, to make invidious comparisons with the familiar. Foreignness in a new country visited, is a different concept for her, more akin to mere difference and thus somehow less alien. Some of that has thankfully rubbed off on me; probably not enough. I was born on an island after all.

One of the purposes of harmonious travel is surely to fit in as much as possible and not stand out as an out-of-towner merely passing through. But it still takes an act of will, to break ice with locals, particularly for anally retentive males such as me who do not like seizing the opportunity to ask directions (a.k.a. admitting to being lost). It is an atavistic fact that most males eschew asking the way since our ancestors' time when killing mammoths required an innate sense of directional geography to know the quickest route to the quarry, places of safety and the way home.

Women tend to be much better at this direction-interrogative and barring a few sociopaths from whom they should quickly absent themselves, they invariably have success at opening wider conversations. Relationships start that way and Sylvie is much better at it than me. I find myself circling back to initially embarrassing encounters in foreign cities where Sylvie's enquiries for directions have turned into conversations about where we are from, what the weather is doing and so on - the lubricants of initial contact. In shops, she is particularly adept at getting assistants to relate beyond the sales patter and I watch in wonder as elaborations of reaching out, flower into something more colourful.

Sing for your supper

As an impoverished student of the late sixties and early seventies, I relied a lot on people who knew people in far off places. The level of hospitality offered was often humbling. In

Alabama, Brisbane and Camp's Bay, Cape Town, and throughout the rest of the locational alphabet, I was invited to, or otherwise scaffed a welcome, a meal or even a bed for the night. This often required some singing for my supper relating travel tales to entertain hosts, but it also afforded a rich seam of opportunity to get to know people and break some ice. Later, it also served well to persuade me to be less stiff upper-lipped and British when breaking into other languages.

This tradition of the traveller as storyteller is an essential way to behave in at least two cultures distant from each other in miles but close in understanding. Maoris and the Welsh both place great store by a visitor telling stories, speaking poetry and even singing (literally) for their supper. I understand something similar exists in Scandinavian cultures. Perhaps it has something to do with the climate there – long dark winter nights and the need for entertainment? Visitors are on show and provided the opportunity is not milked to bore people to death, the invitation to give something of yourself should be accepted with grace. Impressions work two ways.

Travel light
Apart from the obvious practicalities of avoiding excess baggage charges and being able to run for a train or bus, travelling light is an attitude of mind. There is hardly anywhere in the world now where you cannot buy the essentials of survival, water and food obviously, but also maps, first aid kits, needles and thread, shoes and extra clothing etc, so why not seek them out when needed? It is not as if we are now under exchange control conditions that used to prevail when leaving Britain in the 1950s and 1960s – fifty pounds being the top limit for years. Buying essentials might well turn out to be cheaper abroad and finding them will be precisely the exercise necessary to start meeting the

locals. And the inevitable misunderstandings and failures will be well worth their price as you break more ice.

It might just help blend in better as well, particularly where the extra clothing is concerned. We are all familiar with the white-socked and sandaled British tourist, a silly hat and shorts rarely worn by locals in the know, a walking sartorial affront, standing out like a creature from another planet. Apart, that is, from the next one, looking too much the same and classifying both as part of a Dad's Army of aliens for the locals to laugh at behind their hands. Buying a few clothes locally, having first observed the styles a bit, might help the blending process, not to mention the local economy, or at least those of Vietnam or Bangladesh where the garments were probably made. If you buy at *Primark* before leaving, it was probably made in Vietnam or Bangladesh anyway.

Those that travel super-equipped with every necessity are a bit like *Brian the Snail* in the 1960s children's favourite, *The Magic Roundabout*. I recall Brian as the stay-at-home type always alarmed by *Dougal*, the mad shaggy dog who ran around manically looking for new experiences, egged on by the bouncing *Zebedee*. *Ermintrude the Cow* was Brian's soul mate preferring her comfort zone of chewing the cud. *The Magic Roundabout* had cult status by the end of the 1960s, especially for fans of the laid-back hippy, *Dylan the Rabbit*, for whom any movement seemed an unnecessary expenditure of energy while he strummed his guitar.

But *Brian the Snail* is not a character whom those intent on meeting new people or visitors to other countries and even the next village, should emulate. Carrying your home on your back is a bit like taking your culture with you and, for me at any rate, not the right way to do things. Okay, so it may be too much to expect to sleep under the stars, but being prepared to accept temporary homes elsewhere, not always in shiny-shelled hotels is surely the better way to appreciate the differences. Vives les différences! Toujours!

Learn some of the language

When I started travelling to non-anglophone countries, English was not quite the dominant force that it has now become. Things were changing rapidly, but you would still not find good English speakers in business outside the biggest cities in Algeria or Morocco, Bolivia, or Brazil, Thailand, or Malaysia. It meant that some grasp of a local language, luckily still European in North Africa or Latin America but still not English, was essential, on the most basic level.

This requirement is now less and less acute, as English is by far the most common second language spoken worldwide. But we mother tongue anglophones should never forget that it is not the mother tongue of most people that we will meet abroad. Indeed, more people have probably learned English out of necessity than from their mothers. This will come as a surprise to many anglophones whose inability to speak other tongues is legendary among non-English mother tongue speakers. Of course, locals will want to practice their English on you and that may come as an initial relief to the traveller, but it soon becomes a one-way street of cultural exchange. Try, however haltingly, to inject some understanding of local language into the exchange – even if only single words or phrases. The effect is like turning on a light because you are extending a gesture of equality to underwrite friendship and thus a route to meaningful connection.

By good fortune and much unavoidable exposure, I have not suffered from the phobia for languages, at least since meeting people face-to-face. Learning French and a little German at school and university was the usual painful process that so many others will remember. It got me almost nowhere because it was mainly taught so badly and without imagination, a lot of the time. But mainly, it was because rote teaching beyond some valuable grammar tips, was wholly out of context with how languages are normally used. Immersion in everyday discourse, just as in one's mother tongue in childhood, is really the only way to tackle other languages, together with a pre-disposition not to be embarrassed by making mistakes. They are part of the process of getting to know people, and one that inserts humanity and humour into the exchange, all part of building relations.

It also helps to work on the pronunciation a bit. Many of us Anglos apply a British, American, Australian etc, accented interpretation of foreign sounds, such that they come out completely unintelligible in either the source or destination language. The words may be right but the sound is all wrong and it is sounds that matter. Try to suppress the Thames estuary or northern glottal-stopped English, the Bronx drawl or Ranfurly rant when seeking to pronounce local place names or common vocabulary. The difference in local recognition will be immediate.

The fact that English is so much more common than fifty years ago, should not be an excuse to abandon other languages. It behoves us English speakers more than ever to show inclination to reach out to others. Speaking someone else's tongue is to extend a hand of friendship and the reaction will be so much more favourable than those of us who merely repeat what we have said slowly or more loudly, in English. Sadly, there are far too many who still do this – a form of cultural imperialism of which we are barely aware. Watch how people's eyes light up as you try to say something, especially something polite, in their native tongue and the meaningful connections are born.

Try to be a visitor not a tourist

Tourists bring wealth to the economies of many parts of the world that sometimes have few other assets with which to trade. That does not mean they are always welcome and there are now businesses in cities in Europe, for example in Barcelona and Venice, who actively want to limit numbers of trippers because their sheer volume is changing the character of these places for ever. Biting the hand that feeds them perhaps, but it is understandable if you stand on the Ramblas in down town Barcelona, or watch the massive cruise ships glide past the end of St Mark's Square in Venice, bringing thousands more people when they dock.

It helps if the tourist passing through can have some awareness of how they are perceived and might then be able to do something about it. Avoiding the crowds and seeking out lesser-known things to do or see is a good start but being something other than the archetypal tourist would be better still. Work, volunteer, write or research – anything but mere sightseeing - is my mantra. That way, the visitor will be viewed by the hosts as different, but no longer necessarily as unwelcome as the thundering herd of those rubber-necking the local attractions.

If there is a motive for the locals to get engaged in the curiosity of the visitor, a new bond is formed. I have witnessed this many times, through multiple overseas projects, because I was lucky enough to be an interested visitor engaged in something other than tourism. In my case, it was planning and developing new towns and urban infrastructure, subjects in which the host population have lots of vested interest and opinions. It did not take long for the ice to be broken, for differences between host and guest to disappear and lasting relationships to be formed.

Having a shared task to perform, rapidly breaks down the foreignness of visitors. Indeed, it helps identify solutions because different experience is no longer better or worse, it becomes the potential source of finding ways to do things better. When you start to form teams with a common endeavour, you start to celebrate difference or ignore it altogether, the key to breaking down ignorance and prejudice about difference.

Avoid more than basic research

Some travellers see it as their duty to read endless reference manuals on where they are going, including history, politics and geographical features, as well as the key sights to be fitted into an itinerary. *Lonely Planet* or *Rough Guides* are excellent references but referenced alone, you will merely follow a know-it-all tourist trail. Some reading is essential, but it is likely only to be second-hand impressions, and usually from similar visitors passing through. The essential objective is surely to build one's own impressions of a place, not to pre-judge them with someone else's.

Not all rationing of prior reference is wise. Never rely on maps not drawn by proper cartographers, least of all the appalling diagrams usually sketched out without proper thought in newspapers or tourist brochures. Within these apologies for guidance, where is the north point, detail of other key features you will need for reference and - most important of all - the scale? For me, a good map is indispensable because not knowing what direction to walk in, is as unsettling as blundering around in the dark.

Good maps are also neutral conveyors of information that, if detailed enough and read properly, will tell you a great amount about a place and therefore, its people without the editorial of the latest tour guide or travel writer. If you know how to interpret them, detailed maps of a town or city will convey a great deal about why and how the place grew up and how it now works for its inhabitants. Intelligent interpretation of maps of countries will tell you an unexpected amount about the politics, economics and relationships with their neighbours. A lot of history was determined by geography as Tim Marshall relates so graphically in his excellent *Prisoners of Geography: Ten Maps that tell you everything you need to know about Global Politics*. Make maps your priority before travelling from such wonderful stores as Stanfords in London or Vieux Campeurs in Paris.

Leave prejudices at home

It is far too easy to travel or meet people with a set of preconceptions of what or who we will find. Knowing better how to do things is an abiding sin and needs careful management, if not strangling at birth. It is often accompanied by invidious comparison. 'Oh, we do that differently where we come from!' may be rare as an outright offensive statement, but it remains a very common private reaction. It needs suppressing, because the context of why things are different is too complex to allow the comparison to stand.

Let me take up a simple comparison with complex overlaying explanations for the differences; complex because that is exactly what human culture is made of – multiple overlays of circumstance, history and experience. I choose to make the point using the contrasting attitude to alcohol between Scandinavian countries, Russia or Finland, and those surrounding parts of the Mediterranean such as Italy, France and Spain.

Winters are very long and dark in northern latitudes and the summers, correspondingly limited in duration with a few short months when daylight lasts for twenty hours or more. Grain is also the primary source of alcohol because of the cold climate, so alcohol content in the local tipple is usually high.

Coping with the depression caused by daylight deprivation (or maybe making it worse?) during winter, and celebrating the summer, places a very strong priority on alcoholic lubricant for sociability. Light and warmth are human needs for us all and in northern climes, they often have to be artificially induced.

The capacity for drinking in such northern places has, therefore, become well known. Many people there have developed hard heads, and accordingly, problems of alcoholism are widespread. However, it is physical circumstances that have probably brought this about, not the inherent character of the people - Geographical determinism rules.

In Italy, Greece, Spain, Portugal and much of Latin America by contrast, the winters are shorter, warmer and lighter while the dominant source of alcohol is the grape. Thus, celebrating does not need to be so rushed or fevered, neither compensating for light deprivation nor because there won't be another warm day tomorrow. Grape-based alcohol tends to be milder and thus, drunk in a more leisurely manner and with lesser effects on the brain. This is sometimes reflected philosophically by a mañana concept, railed against by frantic northerners who believe - wrongly - that everyone from those southern climes is similarly infected. If they are, it may be because there is less urgency to life's obligations when tomorrow's weather may be as good as that of today.

Here then, are two contrasting philosophies, determined by physical differences fundamental to the contrasting lifestyles between southern and northern latitudes. Take all this into account and prejudices about Scandinavian obsessions with the seasons, timekeeping and alcoholism, or the laid-back mañana attitudes of some Latin peoples, gets put into proper context. If you understand why something is the way it is, it makes you more tolerant about those contrasts with your own values.

Another way of expressing this is to remember the principle of Tim Marshall's book quoted previously, and not forget the power of geography to determine our lifestyles. We are products of our physical and social environments – nature and nurture working together. It explains a lot of national differences that are outside of the immediate control of the majority of citizens. And who would want the world to be the same all over anyway? The world would be a lot more harmonious and remain varied, if everyone understood how differences occur and acted upon that understanding with less ingrained prejudice.

Remain interested as well as interesting

Sadly, curiosity seems to have diminished in our super-connected world. When I started travelling and meeting people in far off places, the jet age was well and truly with us, but there was still a strangeness to new places seen, and others at home wanted to hear about them. I recall on returning from my trip round the US and Canada in 1969, being interviewed about my travels for Radio Wales on the platform at Swansea station. Okay, I hear you thinking, Wales was a bit more parochial than many other places in those days, but the curiosity was warming. It was still an unusual thing to have done at the time and people wanted to hear about it – especially the Woodstock pop festival that year.

Now, so many more people are blasé about long and even short distance travel as the world has shrunk in terms of our mental geography. Some would say you hardly need to travel at all, and maybe to save our planet from more CO_2 emissions, we should pay voluntary tariffs, if not taxes, to do so. (I do; probably not enough). Hopefully, electric planes will be arriving soon to solve this conundrum, because to travel far and wide, or merely over the garden wall into the next street and experience other contexts and cultures, is to understand not only the differences in the world, but also to appreciate that we are all a common species with remarkable similarities to counter the contrasts. That, at least, is a reason to make journeys and nourish the philosophy of connectedness that they engender.

If visiting new places loses its appeal, cling fast at least, to the stimulus of meeting new people. Finding new friendships should be the daily nourishment of all young people and it remains the best medicine for old age. If you are tired of meeting new people, you are probably tired of life.

Don't believe everything you hear - Embrace difference

As for reading about new places, so for making your own judgements about people you meet. I am always wary of people telling me, "You will get on so well with so and so," or the opposite, "Oh, I would steer clear of so and so, if I were you." Fine, you have notice of what one other person thinks of someone else, but while your closest friend's best judgement may be something to trust, it is no guarantee. I find that there is a peculiar but reassuring rule about meeting people that personal chemistries are unique. The ingredients of likes and dislikes are so many and varied, not to mention the circumstances and context of where, when and how you might actually encounter them, that there is no sure way to predict how a new one will work. Be cautious about other people's predictions.

True, there are a few psychopaths in the world and some people so devoid of basic sociability that they invite a near universal conclusion to be worth avoiding. However, for the great majority of humanity, we should assume that each one-to-one encounter will take its own course and not be determined by what others think. Consider the alternative: the world would pretty soon coagulate, like iron filings near a magnet, into groups of overbearing extroverts and self-effacing introverts, wild enthusiasts for anything new, tired cynics who have seen it all before and remain unimpressed by anything, optimistic jokers and serious types who need to get a life. And so on; every extreme of human behaviour, but all of it, amassed in ghettoes of the same behaviour types. What a nightmare!

The fact that this does not normally happen is a testament to the appeal of diversity that is at the core of humanity. Diversity is the source of our flexibility in challenging circumstances, the inventiveness to cope in crises, the ability to laugh at the devil when a more rational response might be to quiver with fear; the talent to work in teams recognising the complementary skills of different members and many, many more responses that are the keys to our survival as a species. We thrive because we are different.

In short, celebrate the diversity of our species and try to take everyone you meet at face value or something approaching that, until they present evidence to the contrary. Make this a personal mission for you and you alone to take the world and its people as you find them, not as filtered through the impressions of others. You are unique - but so is everyone else!

Chapter 10

Getting Along with Nearly Everybody

Meaningful connections can be defined as imaginative identification between individuals - I have some understanding about how you think and react, and you do likewise with me. This concluding chapter addresses the fractures recorded previously and looks at how personal empathy might overcome them.

*

My first six chapters recorded a wide range of examples of where and how society is coming apart. As with any broad social trend, there are exceptions, as individuals and communities push back against the de-personalisation of their connectivity with fellow beings. But technology makes it all too easy to allow relationships to be filtered through, and dominated by, digital devices. I addressed many of the possible indicators of the fracture before roaming through a range of the ways in which human relations have changed through my lifetime, in terms of political discourse, gender relations, how offices dynamics have evolved, perceptions of place and belonging, and hardest of all, coping with trauma. These are key ingredients determining empathy or its absence in how humans relate to, and understand, each other. As we approach the end of the first quarter of the twenty-first century, it makes sense to take stock.

Then, I spent some time explaining how critical it is to understand context, such that one person's interpretation of events or circumstances will differ from another's, very often based on tiny variations of disposition, mood, or what may have happened in the minutes or seconds before any appraisal were possible. I then described my own upbringing and early forming of views of the world before presuming to offer some advice via an encounter guide for meeting new people and circumstances. Pre-disposition, as my context chapter described, is critical to positive responses to new stimuli whether physical or psychological.

Now, I want to move on perhaps to the most important chapter of all, where I suggest ways to mend the fractures we are experiencing in society. Not surprisingly by now, these rely on understanding and expressing empathy in how we live our lives and interact with each other.

Human talent for adapting

Can the fractures ever be fixed? Yes, our species needs to remember how flexible we can be! Only when necessity dictates, do we realise that the actions, environments and positions we previously adopted were merely passing behaviours and that we can change not only to survive but to thrive. We spend a lot of time without realising it, in our own comfort bubbles; content that the way things are is the way they will continue. The shock of change is sometimes brutal, but that passes pretty soon and new norms assert themselves with the unavoidable need to adapt.

In response to the pandemic through just a few months of 2020, there have been profound adaptations to the way we live our lives. Most people are now accepting the principle and practice of social distancing and lockdown to an extent hitherto not experienced in most societies since different behaviours, but similar social limitations, were imposed during World War II. Humanity's flexibility to change has already been amply demonstrated to limit an invisible threat. In the process, people have reached out to each other in ways that had become rare or non-existent before, and a real sense of community has often been engendered, especially among and towards health workers, so long undervalued by societies worldwide.

We have combatted dystopias before. The plagues of our so called European middle ages, wiped out huge proportions of the population but the resultant scarcity of labour that had survived, gave the lowliest peasant the first sense of their real worth. Wages and working conditions took a long time to improve but we can trace their commencement on that journey from these disasters.

The Great Enlightenment of the late eighteenth century was felt variously but profoundly across Europe and North America. Educated people, followed progressively by the masses as they became better informed, saw the decline of autocratic monarchies replaced progressively by more democratic parliamentary systems. Material optimism was boosted by the widespread belief that an industrial revolution, combined with other advances of science and technology, would soon release man from much of the drudgery of brute labour. Luddites and some religious fundamentalists resisted by attacking the machinery either literally or metaphorically, but the broad outlook followed the technical trajectory towards a materially better world. Das Kapital, as the first communist manifesto, arrived in 1867 as a justifiable check on the worst forms of capitalist greed, and rightfully recorded that it would be a very long time, if ever, before the proletariat would see the benefits. But like so many other political movements, its followers fell far short of its ideals, while slowly, the proletariat did emerge from the worst forms of exploitation. Those assuming the duty to promote communist principles steadily allowed themselves to be corrupted by the maintenance of power before ideology. And power corrupts.

But change and improvements to the lot of the masses did come and have continued, as we adapted from an agrarian and widely self-sufficient lifestyle to an urban, consumerist and therefore interdependent one. There are many parts of the world where exploitation amounting to near slavery still prevails in labour markets, but again, as after the industrial revolutions within the first national economies to undergo change, these excesses will slowly be rooted out and replaced with better conditions.

If you thought my examples of human adaptation were too global for specific application, consider two countries that transformed themselves after military, economic and social defeat and destruction in the middle of the last century. Germany and Japan were arguably the strongest military powers in the world only four years prior to their complete collapse in defeat at the end of World War II in 1945. Yet, within a decade, they, or at least West rather than East Germany, had re-built their industrial economies, transformed their education systems and adopted democratic forms of government. All this, despite highly intrusive previous leadership regimes which had taught the population never to question supreme authority and subject themselves entirely to the will of the state. External aid, enlightened guidance, personal sacrifice and prodigiously hard work were the ingredients, but none of these were as important as the initial motivation to adapt and change national philosophy.

Consider also, the impacts to two great novels during the mid-twentieth century, *Brave New World*, first published in 1932 and *1984*, published in 1948. Their authors Huxley and Orwell respectively, portrayed strikingly similar images of social control that they claimed, at the time, were only a few years into the future. What they wrote about, either side of the Second World War, was widely recognised as a realistic threat to free society, and most were repelled by the possible consequences. It took a six-year war and millions of lives to achieve this against fascist and Nazi versions of social control, and a further forty-five more, to do the same with the way communism was being interpreted to dictate terms between state and people. For me, these ideologies were little different to each other, full of self-styled noble objectives, but corrupted to the pursuit and retention of personal power, extending to mass extinctions of parts of the population who happened not to fit the ideology.

The autocracies were for a brief period, at the end of the twentieth and beginning of the twenty-first centuries, in decline. We now know that Francis Fukuyama's book *The End of History and the Last Man* from the early 1990s, was premature in suggesting that the decline of bi-polar confrontation would also usher in the triumph of capitalist, if not wholly social, democracy. But there was a strong sense, particularly in those countries that had cast off the yoke of previous communist regimes, that things could only get better.

Sadly, with the resurgence of nationalist rather than collectivist principles in recent years, the autocracies of the last century have not been replaced with open democracies but rather too many kleptocracies. Kleptocracies, because whatever ideology they lay claim to, if any, they end up hell bent on the enrichment and aggrandizement of the individuals holding power in each. Such governing systems do not amount to political philosophies and perhaps the only difference between the last century and this, is that no one bothers any more to dress up their governing style under the banner of a political ideology. They are merely age-old personal greed, selfishness and retention of power, often portrayed as nationalism and clothed in the national flag. I think we all know what and who they really are, but early recognition of when it starts happening is still a challenge.

But the process of human adaptation goes on. Just now, a silent majority of citizens of many kleptocratic regimes have turned away from civic engagement, focusing on family and friends as the only sphere of influence where they can hope to improve their lives. Knowing they can change very little; the average citizens have switched off. But that too is adapting. When they perceive a sea change in their society's politics, a return to democratic accountability and transparency, they usually react positively. Sadly, with insufficient lasting success so far, we have observed these trends often in recent years, in the Arab Spring across many Middle Eastern countries, in Ukraine and most recently, in Byelorussia.

Just now, as I observed previously, it is populism that dominates political thinking – the adoption of an identity, based viewpoint that tolerates little alternative and a view of the world that limits itself squarely within self-interest – What's in it for me? Ideologies that look towards wider community benefit are in retreat, but this still amounts to adaptation to external circumstances and we will adapt again.

Notice me, notice me!

One of the wellsprings of populism has been the apparent absence of respect afforded to those with little power to influence events from those that do. Looked at another way, self-respect is partly dependent on the recognition of others, but it is pretty much essential for offering it back, in turn. It is mutual and it is cyclical. This can be explored at the highest statesmanlike or diplomatic level, based on a scholarly grasp of history and geopolitics but let me explain it in a far more parochial vernacular.

Wales, the place of my birth, is a small country, set via conquest rather than treaty, over seven hundred years ago, within a much larger one that eventually, became the UK. Wales has had little enough recognition in the world as the first definable linguistic conquest of the English language. When the

Welsh language started to disappear, so inevitably, over many generations, did the parts of its culture that depended on the spoken word. As I stated before, I am no nationalist for things overtly Welsh, so I paid all of this little heed until I went to school just over the border into England, where being Welsh was a label to be worn with good humour, whether you wanted it or not. I like, but have no excessive pride in, my fellow Welsh people. They seem just as prone to human weakness as any other small group. But being branded by a thundering herd of the English neighbours, tended to engender loyalty to a tribe with whom I previously thought I was only lightly connected. Faced with a mild threat, we all hunker down regardless of origins.

This Celtic tribal loyalty is invariably dealt with through humour, and a play on parochialism that is our national specialty. Most of it goes straight over the heads of our near, dear neighbours, and that is precisely its point. Such is the discrepancy of scale and influence between Wales and England that much of Welsh identity is wrapped around little more than not being the same as them. Probably suits both.

For most Welsh people, maintenance of national pride is still likely to be determined not through the ballot box but on the sports field. In Wales, that usually means rugby union. So, when we can beat the national selection of our big neighbour, chosen from their pool of players over ten times the size of ours, we are more than satisfied. Since these encounters started in the 1880s, the win honours have been broadly equal, despite the hugely disproportionate numbers of potential contestants on either side, not to mention the discrepancy in financial resources available to each. That is just the way we like it, because in the end, it is fifteen vs. fifteen on the field. Not for nothing does the answer to the question as to "What time is kick off?" include the reminder to, "Bring your boots, just in case you're needed, see!"

Most Welsh people would die happy scoring the winning try at Twickenham, better still, in Cardiff.

We are proud of being the thin red line. Rugby is one of the few occasions when the English have to take Wales seriously, given the former's sad disposition to ignore or take differences for granted and the latter's desperate desire to be noticed and counted as unique - just like everyone else. Respecting people's desire to be noticed is one of the first rules of connecting with them.

I use a traditional sporting metaphor not just to bang on about Welsh rugby prowess. Far more important, is the need to show that for most people, self-respect emanates from the respect of others. If that is openly offered and generously returned, we would all learn to live together more harmoniously. We might even accept defeat at rugby a bit more readily. Well no, perhaps I should not go that far.

There is a lesson here for the waxing and waning of empires and their resultant conflicts. If the rulers of empires could have spared a little more respect for those that they ruled, wars to dominate and eventual struggles to re-separate, would be less. Harmonious co-existence could flourish all the more.

Sport offers an alternative to more serious competitiveness, including war. But that is not all. At the personal level, and quite apart from the physical health benefits, there are huge social ones. And mental health is very much bound up in connecting both together. We need to encourage young people out of their digital bubbles to exercise their minds, as well as their bodies.

You may say that there is nothing more mind expanding than working with the Internet, but we also need variety of ingredients for all round health. The endorphins released by physical activity have a powerful benefit for the brain as well. So, it does not matter what form it takes; football, tennis, swimming, mountain walking and many more (including even rugby), but joining a sports club and getting outside to enjoy physical exercise and the mental stimulus of like-minded company, has almost no downside, as far as I can see. And one of the best benefits might just be another dimension for getting noticed and respected.

Routes to greater social awareness

Despite recent populist setbacks, there is no reason for us to assume that the ills of our self-centred society to which I referred in my first chapter, cannot be corrected. Excessive dependence on digital technology in general and its messaging software, in particular, may have been a recent cause of greater dissonance in society. But it might be possible to apply some control of their use to promote understanding that face-to-face connections are needed for meaningful human relations to thrive. We need to re-discover how to build empathy and social awareness with our fellow men and women. Simple? Well let's see.

The key to this is expanding our horizons in terms of awareness of who might be there and what is to be discovered beyond our immediate neighbourhood - 'Getting over the garden wall', as in my mother's homily to me when young. It takes curiosity to learn and experience new stimuli on a human level; easily said, more difficult to achieve. Broadening the mind could be defined as coming to understand why people behave in a particular way, hold certain opinions or react to given situations as they do. Empathy with an individual's perception of society, amounts to genuine social awareness. It will help predict how strangers might behave, what opinions might be encountered, and how people are likely to react before a given situation develops. How liberating is that? To be able through experience, to anticipate people's reactions the better to get to know them on a meaningful basis; in short, not seeming so strange to strangers.

I firmly believe that exposing oneself to other cultures is one of the best ways to develop empathy and understanding – not just by getting to know people, but working with and if possible, living among them. For real insight, raising families together or living as neighbours, might attain the necessary familiarity through everyday language and study of individual habits and behaviours. This all takes time and is likely impossible with more than one culture at a time, but there are lots of examples of how it can happen.

Why would you want to achieve empathy rather than mere tolerance and understanding? Quite apart from the satisfaction of human relationships taken to a higher level, there are incalculable material benefits in finding empathy. For a start, it is the single most valuable device in the briefcase of any diplomat or businessman. Dealing with other countries or enterprises offers great benefits but only lastingly so if there is mutual benefit. Anything more one-sided can never last; those that lose out will always be looking for compensation. Knowing what is mutually beneficial, calls for understanding of the other person's agenda and thus knowing while negotiating, when to give ground and when to stand fast.

Anyone claiming they will not give ground as part of their claim to lead any negotiation is playing to a credulous gallery. They also demonstrate that they know nothing about how negotiation works. A combination of holding fast and giving ground is part of the toolkit when anticipating a protagonist's response to a set of moveable positions.

The world statesmen or women I would always admire would be those who worry excessively about what their protagonist gets out of each deal, not what they are getting for their own side of the argument. They are the ones who know that only mutual benefits make arrangements work in the long term. The result of such mutual agreements might even generate peace and harmony between nations, or at least, avoid war. There is not much more important in the affairs of men than that.

Body language for when speech isn't enough

The benefits of learning other languages are self-evident as the most basic building block towards understanding. Speaking someone else's tongue is to extend a hand of friendship, regardless of the mistakes you might make in the process. Indeed, limited language ability can also be an advantage. Deaf and blind people develop acute faculties to compensate for their loss of hearing or sight - deafness often granting the skill of perceptive observation - while blind people frequently have the most acute hearing. Applying a similar principle, inability to understand a conversation can sometimes be replaced by accurate observation of body language. It is astonishing how much you can learn without understanding a word, but from tone of voice, posture, juxtaposition of movement, chosen seating patterns at a meeting, but more than anything else, facial expression.

Of the six-hundred and fifty muscles in the human body, there are only forty three in the face, but perhaps because they are so small, they combine to provide an almost infinite range of expressions that only the most skilled communicator can hide. Stranger still is the fact that only six muscles control eye movement while as many as seventeen control the lips. Learning a bit about what facial expressions are engendered by critical sentiments such as scepticism or doubt, irritation, rising anger, wry amusement or acquiescence and approval, often reveals more about what is going on in someone's mind then merely hearing what people say. Recognizing these signs is so much better than looking at emojis. Words can often send the wrong signals and given that what people do, is always more important than what they say, body language observance will always be critical to empathy. You will not get this from texting.

Breaking out of the comfort zone

As I observed in the previous chapter on encountering new people and places, finding connections with people and gaining empathy through travel often requires journeying alone, leaving oneself open to fresh human company and physical impressions not so easily gained while travelling within the comfort zone of friends or family. I have always been a bit reluctant to travel in groups. You carry a too familiar frame of reference with you like a snail carrying his home on his back. That is no way to journey. You must go with an open mind and be ready to sleep under the stars - okay, only literally perhaps in my twenties in Australia or the Sahara, but metaphorically speaking now and forever - accepting and welcoming what crosses your path.

Of course, mostly everyone has his or her limits of tolerance to the overload of new experience from which to retreat into the balm of the familiar. But open-mindedness is crucial to avoid the trap of lazy ignorance that precursors the inability to process new experience. We are not good at this in Britain, perhaps a function of island status; we know what we like. Also, while there is plenty of evidence of prejudice in other cultures as well, we need to tackle our own before getting ready to point out such weakness in others. Finding meaningful connections with others surely starts with questioning one's own standpoint before trying to identify the strengths and weaknesses in others.

Here's another example of getting out of one's comfort zone. Like most people I know, I tend to read a newspaper because I recognize the journalists' writing and know my way around. But really, for the purposes of stimulating my brain's judgement faculty, I should try to read newspapers with which I disagree, the ones that take me out of my comfort zone. Surely, the purpose of developing a point of view is to measure it against another – usually with some dissent but all in the spirit of cognition and debate? Sadly, most people have read one newspaper - if they still read one at all - through most of their lives. You can tell because they often become a conversational mirror of its contents. Comfort zones are not a good place for any length of time, to sustain an enquiring mind.

Reviewing how places work

As a geographer and urbanist, I probably view the world slightly differently to people with different career backgrounds. I am always looking at why a place works or does not, measured against various prosaic but fundamental factors such as transport, environmental management, ease of water supply, population growth or decline etc. When working on a client's project, this becomes a bit formulaic, because a master plan for a new community, industrial complex or future land use policy must be generated as an end result. But even when I am visiting as a tourist, I often apply these faculties subconsciously. As often as not and despite much practice, I get my analysis wrong, but it does not stop me trying.

This professional place review to give it a grand title, is usually restricted to physical evidence; I usually consider the social and community issues to be far too complex to call without a lot more evidence not readily available at first pass. For example, growing communities are by and large healthy ones, as people flock to where there is work, and where things function effectively, if not always fairly. The shanty towns and informal housing areas which accommodate a growing proportion of the world's urban poor, particularly in countries with limited planning restrictions, are among the most fascinating neighbourhoods and communities for an urbanist to study. Left to themselves, without interference of municipal authorities and their attendant professional planners, architects and engineers, the physical infrastructure of such communities would evolve successfully on its own. That might hold true until the inhabitants seek formalized electric power, water and sewage treatment systems, against which city authorities might trade long term occupational rights reciprocated by the right to charge municipal taxes. Negotiating between these two interests and the groups representing each amount to one of the most fascinating processes in community planning. Perhaps anthropology is the key to success?

A lot of urban planners working in the developing world, espouse a self-help model in response to informal edge of city building, "Let the people develop in their own way with a little peripheral help," being their mantra – "They are solving their own housing crisis." Given that more formalized industrial building processes are largely unavailable to new urban arrivals, such communities are left to operate a largely market-oriented system of day-to-day welfare and control. Goods and services are often traded between people on a barter rather than formal money exchange basis. Shanty-town dwellers are usually there because there is work nearby, and they are earning money to support not just themselves but also relations elsewhere, until the two can be reunited. They understand the ways of the market better than most. Allocation of living space and building materials may seem disorganized, but usually work on a free market basis, and sometimes via groups or individuals operating at the edge of the law.

City authorities sometimes have to work more closely with leaders of shanty-town communities than they would like, accepting that the self-help principle to facilitate access to building materials is the only solution. The provision of physical (e.g. water supplies) and social (e.g. schools) services comes later in exchange for the payment of taxes. This is no more than working with the grain of how things operate; municipal authoritarianism of either leftward or rightward inclination rarely works with informal but very vibrant communities.

My point with all this talk of urban planning is that left to themselves, communities usually find ways to organize themselves. The idea that anarchy is the result could not be further from the truth. Law and order may be applied arbitrarily, but if a long-term view of justice is taken, by and large, it exists through the need to co-exist. And there are rules – spoken or unspoken - about how people must behave for the community to work. We could learn a lot from watching how illegal housing areas across the world evolve. They are closer to the way cultures enable community than those of us from more settled environments might realise. And they are living proof of the adaptability of our species.

I believe that this working with the grain of things is fundamental to developing empathy and understanding. Experiencing new cultures while continuing to live, breathe and broadcast the merits of one's own seems to me a foolish notion bordering on arrogance. We British were especially effective at this in times of empire with negative results. There were – maybe still are - those who believe that one's integrity is under threat if you go native, a phrase that implies for me, a sense of superiority in the visitor that will make him or her especially impervious to new sensations.

I do not advocate that newcomers should completely embrace host cultures. It would take too much time to absorb every nuance and subtle shift of habits and values, and anyway ensure that you stood out as neither fish nor fowl. But some recognition, that, 'Things are done differently around here', is essential for the sensitive traveller through space and time and critical to being received with an open welcome, rather than indifference or hostility.

Such pragmatism to work with the grain, influences my politics in the developed world as well. If it works, leave it be and place the ideology second.

Has my ideology evolved through life? Not really!

My politics is probably slightly conservative (small 'c' definitely) probably owing something to an awareness that for every action, there will be a reaction, and the greater the former, the more extreme the latter. One pace forward and two back, accepting the principle that more often than not, less happens in politics from action than from reaction. There is no point in espousing extreme solutions to governance because someone will always push back with interest. That much is evident from even the most rudimentary study of history.

With the final collapse in the last decade of the twentieth century of an avowedly communist system, in almost all societies, ideology has become far less important to good government than the enduring principle of enlightened leadership. Identity whether with culture or individuals has also taken over from ideologies as these are shown to be corruptible though power. People and individuals at the top of a political party are what matter more than their espoused ideology or cause. Events are what dominate the governing agenda rather than high ideals. And dealing with events is difficult enough.

While this may seem cynical, it is still a value system judged on fair play. I think most people, regardless of culture, historical context and experience, understand inherently what is meant by fair play, though there is a fond nostalgia in Britain for our having invented it through sport. Did we always practice what we preached? Not always.

I also believe that prescriptive political ideologies may have been suited to a simpler time of relations between rulers and the governed but are ineffective in a heterogeneous era of multi-cultural communities and multiple communication media. Who for example, one hundred years ago would have imagined that the greatest threat to personal freedom would not be a political ideology different from their own, but rather cyber-controlled data? Would they have also gone on to reflect that the greatest opportunity for democratic accountability would also be that same digital media? One hundred years ago, very few of us could have imagined the world of hyper communication that we now inhabit, being so used to the fact that accurate information was hard to come by at all. Now, we have plenty of information, but we have just as much trouble as before in determining if it is accurate. We need to spend as much time understanding the source of information as its content.

How can you wholly embrace any ideology in such a fast-changing technical world? Better to adopt pragmatic principles of doing the best for the largest possible number of people, while keeping a wary eye on those who seek to lead, including these days, those in the communications industry. They control what is said and in what way it is edited. Opinion influencers are as pivotal to good government as those who make the decisions. They need watching closely.

At their extremes of course, autocratic governments claiming either left or right leanings become one and the same thing, namely pursuers of personal aggrandizement once in possession of power through suppression, openly or covertly of those who do not have it. Fascists, communists and demagogues of no particular ideology, except egotism, deployed the same tactics of suppression of the individual; their ideologies always defaulting to the single pursuit of social control. If I espouse any ideology, it is a bit libertarian - to promote individual freedom of expression and resist autocratic behaviour of any stripe. I hope that is not the purest form of anarchy, but if I am intolerant of any one thing, it is intolerance.

Overall, most things that stop war have got to be good. There are limits of course, as my parents' generation came to realize at the end of the 1930s. But there are very few bellicose situations that do not share out justice and blame in almost equal measures. More subtly, anything that acts as a release to frustrations about the perceived inferiority or superiority of one group of people over another has got to be similarly beneficial.

I have voted at one time or another for all three mainstream British political parties: Conservative, Labour and Liberal and their various offshoots. I have never had time for any of the extremes to the right or left of these three, nor even the nationalist siren calls that started in our Celtic countries and are now reflected in England too. For me, the political movements that espouse a breaking up of our island union have cultivated a fashionable independence philosophy in the name of greater cultural identity. I see this as no more than a desire to be noticed as different from the mainstream (predominantly English) culture and to that extent, it is entirely understandable.

Whether they admit to it or not, too much of the nationalist cause is shaped around the negative of, "We are not English." But we English, Scots, Irish or Welsh and those who have joined us more recently from more diverse cultures, have far more in common than we do apart. If only cultural and national respect could be re-engendered, our diversity would afford us – as for many centuries past – a huge source of strength which nationalist identity seeks to erase. Too often, as we saw in Ireland in the early 1920s after independence from Britain, the nationalist groups fall out with each other internally when the initial source of their desire for separation is finally withdrawn. They find the same old ideological differences raising their heads as before and nationalism dissolves into factionalism once again; only diversity is lost.

Something similar has been afoot for us regarding our relations with near neighbours in Europe in recent years. The wellspring of Brexit politics has for me been nationalism, a cry for independence from rather than interdependence with, the affairs and aspirations of those who live close by in mainland Europe. It is dressed up as sovereignty or the brilliant strap line, 'Take back control', as if in our super-connected world, that would ever be fully possible. I believe we will come to realise that the independence we now seek in our hyper-connected world will be illusory and we will need to find common cause again with those who live close by.

In brief, I believe that nationalist sentiment is fundamentally anti-pathetic to understanding others. It seeks to divide when we need to find common cause that is fundamental to human harmony. Faced with a hostile invasion of little green beings from another planet, we would quickly find common cause with our fellow humans with whatever opinions and differences. So why not recognize our common destiny now and learn to get along and thrive together?

So, not much change over four or five decades, might summarize my broad values and politics both home and abroad, and hopefully, this would chime with many readers, if they have accompanied me this far. But what of cultural values, prejudices, preferences and eternal verities transferred with mother's milk (nature) or just the way we do things around here (nurture)? These ingredients of greater or lesser awareness of different ways of life pose tougher questions. Here, I think my lifetime of journeys and the incidental process of seeking empathy has affected me profoundly as it probably affects many others journeying from youthful exuberance and apparent certainty towards a more reflective and uncertain old age.

Wide experience of other geographies, cultures, people and both odd and everyday events happening along the way, presents us with questions such as why we travel, what we seek on the way and whether the elusive empathy gift can be found at the end of the rainbow. Maybe, the question I am asking here is, do we become more certain of things we thought we already knew, or can we change our perspectives on life, based on travel and meeting new people to shift those values we learned in younger age?

Wait a minute. Is that not simply what age offers you? The exuberance of youth replaced by sage reflection, filtered through the wise contemplation of hard-won experience. Why this reverence for age? Mentally speaking, I don't feel any age at all. I want to be more frivolous now than fifty years ago. Back then, creating an impression of sober maturity was necessary to seem credible, while now, I want anything but. Remember that great 1955 photograph of Albert Einstein sticking his tongue out for the camera? Forget the genius bit. I could not aspire to that, but Einstein's sense of mischief is exactly what I want for my ageing years, to shake and sometimes shock comfortable assumptions about what and how people think and behave. All the better to make people I meet look afresh at their own world and themselves.

Re-shaping of values over time

Having travelled the world so extensively over six of my seven decades, do I now view my values differently? Have I found greater empathy working and living among people of other cultures, languages and points of views? And critically, do I see our society as capable of finding again its sense of unity through common cause as human beings relating to each other face-to-face rather than digitally? Like any other writer, I can only answer for myself, but let me examine what has stayed the same and what has changed through seventy years of life and my widespread travels through so many diverse cultures.

I cannot see much change in my values over time, by which I mean, what I like and respect in most people and what makes me inherently mistrustful of a small minority. I don't recall this respect being instilled by parents, but they probably had a discreet hand in it all, as values grew on me like the extra inches of height, absorbed unconsciously through life experience. Parental influence was effective but invisible – the best kind, as I have learned as a parent myself.

However, my prejudices have probably changed from those with which I grew up. Making judgements in ignorance of facts needs a pre-disposition to think you already know better, regardless of the evidence. This is stupid, but it is all too common and probably emanates from not being bothered to find out, or sheer rejection of the unknown that is an alternative to fear, contempt and eventually loathing, for any sort of strangeness.

So that has been a change. I would, for example, once have merely accepted, or even revelled in, the preconceived perceptions of other national cultures - usually negative, because that seemed more fun - German authoritarianism, Italian vanity, American brashness, Spanish pride and so on. Sadly, country areas like the one where I grew up may be more prone to such fixed views than urban ones, because there is less cultural variety around. All outsiders seem strange. But in the best countrymen and women, this is quietly compensated by more time and perhaps interest taken, to understand outsiders and their circumstances more profoundly – empathy pursued through having, and using, the time to listen. Remaining curious to change is a pre-requisite.

In the quiet times of very early morning while still only half awake, I reflect drowsily on such matters. While half asleep, ideas can sometimes seem very clear. Is this the source of Australian Aboriginal dreamtime, deemed in their non-materialist and frequently misunderstood culture to be of equal status as time awake? I am sure that my half-awake reflections are a long way from aboriginal dreamtime, but they sometimes revolve around what it would have been like to have lived a different life back in the place of my birth – one perhaps, where contentment was gained from much simpler values than rushing about the world as I have done, always hungry for the next impressionistic experience. What use all this empathy without the time to savour it and the relationships engendered?

If I had never gone away from Pembrokeshire, the often sleepy place of my birth, I might have found myself living next door to people content in their own skin, just knowing how their own corner of the world was toddling along; the pub and the post office on the corner, what Rhys or Myfanwy were doing with the house down the road and whether the weather is set fair or coming on to rain. I can hear them now … "How you been keeping? Why aye boy, mustn't grumble, fair to middlin'!" spoken in that wonderful west Wales lilt, a hybrid of Welsh and west country, perhaps containing more wisdom about time passing and things all being the same tomorrow, than any fevered quest by me for deeper meaning or insight. The hiraeth is very strong sometimes.

Do such people have a wiser take on life? Will they meet their end more serenely than those of us who cannot keep still? I cannot say, but sometimes when recounting with such friendly company, tales of adventure or strange experience in a far off place (anywhere east of Carmarthen for the true Pembrokeian), there is a look in the eye of such tranquil souls, as if to ask, 'Do you really find your God through such thrashing about the world?'. I cannot answer this convincingly, but for me, choosing to leave such a contented place was an act of commitment to a different way of being. However much I love to go back, it would have driven me nuts if I had stayed. The empathy that I sought with my fellow man had to be on a wider scale.

Love, life and the pursuit of happiness

Returning to the themes of my Prologue, what are the ingredients that need to be re-discovered to achieve greater world harmony, perhaps summed up as the qualities of love, life and the pursuit of happiness? As I identified towards the end of my chapter on trauma, Maslow defined the obvious basics - shelter, freedom from threat of violence or other crimes, health and well-being through clean water to drink and absence of threat to food supplies. To move up the levels of need to love, belonging and self-esteem, we need to build meaningful relationships with our fellow humans. I see no alternative to this source of happiness. And only when we have achieved self-esteem, can we hope to attain the highest level of need in life of realizing our full potential? Perception of having achieved that without the foundations below it, is building one's mental self-confidence on sand. This holds good for society, as much as for the individual.

Easier said than delivered of course, but throughout my career, I have tried to play a small part in development projects that addressed some of those basic needs, the better for those communities to develop for themselves some of the higher ones as well. For the route to the top of the Maslow pyramid, that of achieving one's own full potential with whatever talents we may possess, the aspirations become more abstract and the journey travelled is pretty much on one's own. Alone but not lonely, because of being surrounded by the self-confidence of a place in the community of friends and family and the support that they bestow.

In my first chapter, I wrote about twin culprits for the high levels of stress that seem to infect too much of society. They were the recent absence of freely available credit with which to assuage the appetite for short term consumerist gratification, and over dependence on digital communication at the expense of face-to-face relationships. Neither drug-like dependency will be easy to overcome. Until about 2009, we had benefitted from about six decades of access to more and more goods and services either via cash or progressively more available credit. Looking back, this represents a lifetime's experience for at least two generations of consumers. This was partly overlain by up to twenty years during which there has been widespread use of the Internet. Consumerism is, therefore, engrained in day-to-day life experience and throughout the living memory of most people. The Internet and its use are heading for similar embedding within human culture. Have we completely forgotten what life was like before each?

Availability of these twin dystopias of consumerism and digital communication can nevertheless be managed better, and education is the key. We must use our judgement faculties brought to us through the widest possible life as well as learning experience, to re-discover how to relate directly to our networks of friends and family. Awareness of this need is the essential first step. Equally, we need to wean ourselves away from excessive consumerism and re-locate our satisfaction in a life less dependent on goods and services delivered to us on a plate.

I wrote towards the end of chapter 1 about the cultural foundations of society – philosophy, art, music, sport and great places to live. Of course, digital communication via the internet has worked wonders for giving us the capacity to develop these foundations on a global scale. Perhaps this globalisation of culture is now an ingredient of bringing humanity closer together as one community, but I am not sure about that. On its own, remote working that is the common component of digital communication, can never replace the depth of understanding that close physical contact with each other engenders. While this is currently challenged by the pandemic, we must strive to re-generate the means to getting us back together physically, so that the stimulus of our creativity can thrive once again.

At the outset of this book, I listed many of the factors which make it such a challenge to achieve meaningful connections with people far away – language, race, perceptions of history, physical environment, politics, poverty vs. riches and gender, all summed up by the generic term, human culture. However, I have found in our time-poor world, that there is one common factor that trumps all others when achieving connections with strangers. It is to identify and work with what is an individual's or a group's agenda for their encounter with you. It is as if they are asking, "What does this newcomer bring me? How are they adding value to my life?" And over what timescale – whether months, weeks, days, and even nowadays, the next ten minutes. The need to include the last of these timescales is a sad reflection on the attention span of people in the modern world, but we have to work with current reality not the one we would like. Ten minutes is often all one gets before judgements are formed. Call it speed dating if you like, but it works at any level of building relations with each other. Miss the vital signals and we will get nowhere; spot them early and the start of meaningful relations can be ours.

Knowing another person's agenda is a critical ingredient of empathy. Consider the benefits of this connection. There are few feelings more empowering than finding common cause with strangers. It is easy enough to agree with people with whom we have grown up, live close to or with whom we have common experience and a mother tongue. But how much more satisfying it is to find that, despite differences of politics, gender, language, history and wider aspects of culture, people can still connect and find common cause across these barriers.

This can take the simplest form of agreeing on a single point or reacting similarly to a given circumstance. For me, making meaningful connections with people has also emerged through my choice of career, master planning and designing new towns where communities have the means to flourish. It is important for we planners to realise that the last of these actions, generating flourishing communities will be a self-help process not one that outsiders can expect to plan successfully. But we can set the physical components in place to enable the flourishing to occur. What a challenge. What satisfaction when you see it starting to work.

Making connections does not need to emerge from such complex objectives, the simplest ones agreeing on just one thing or laughing at the same situation can be just as effective. Ultimately, common cause between individuals, communities and even countries leads to alliances that are stronger precisely for the diversity of those who sign up to them. The ultimate connection is the most elusive of all, common cause between all of humanity's people. Its pursuit is the greatest challenge to us all.

Here then, at the last, is my recipe for reaching out across social distance. Finding meaningful connections with acquaintances and strangers alike is to anticipate what those you meet may be thinking and aspiring to, the better to generate the optimum level of mutual benefit, understanding and harmony. Finding the means to create those conditions has motivated much of my lifetime of journeys from the time when I first reached out across the garden wall and the social distance that I found there. While I am still in the foothills of understanding human nature, my eyes remain wide open. It is as much a beautiful world as when I started my journey through it nearly seventy years ago. Empathy sought, meaningful connections frequently found and fractures repaired.

Epilogue

CV19: An Opportunity

A look at the implications of the CV19 pandemic on society and the issues it raises around the themes of my book.

*

I am now writing this end note as the Coronavirus (CV19) continues to defy observation and predictions about its methods, trajectory and pace of infection. These factors are unique to every geographical, social and economic circumstance it finds among its human victims, making it very hard to draw common conclusions about any two national or even local community experiences. We are rapidly discovering that local contexts far more than broad national or international ones determine patterns of infection and thus the means to limit them. Economic and social impacts are equally diverse, but a series of patterns will emerge with time. None of this has stopped a range of armchair commentators from wading in with every kind of generalisation and critique of how one authority is dealing with the problems either better or worse than the next. Fake news? Probably not, but lots of making up one's mind regardless of all the necessary evidence.

So far so thoroughly bad, but the threats of diseases have been with us as a species since we evolved. And we have coped. What we are learning now about CV19 will be valuable for further application not only to defeat CV19, but against new threats in the future. So, its globalisation is an opportunity as well as threat because there is a huge level of international cooperation to find the best ways to limit spread and find the vaccines.

Within a few months, so much has changed. What used to be a series of slow social and behavioural evolutions, for example remote working away from offices, have just accelerated. Many of these changes are examples of the fractures I examined in my early chapters. What used to be the way we related to people and performed day-to-day functions such as shopping or use of public transport may have been changed or lost forever.

The virtual closing down of large parts of the world economy is unprecedented, with huge swathes of previous industry and commerce undergoing shrinkage through lost demand, and other rapid transformations, even where they have managed to survive. A few sectors have thrived, such as food retail, online services and pharmaceuticals. No one knows for sure how the long-term unemployment impacts will work, or where new business will emerge from the changes now being forced through at unprecedented speed in response to new patterns of demand and supply.

Many now say that the mental health and welfare impacts of the pandemic are likely to be worse than the disease itself and must be responded to by kick-starting the economy, even if this revives the rate of virus spread. There also remain a few deniers of the current state of play, of whom those refusing to wear masks are an obvious example, rejecting contrary evidence as fake news – an ostrich like burying of heads that would have been unlikely before the malign increase of fakery.

Emotionally and psychologically, the cost of the pandemic has been even harder to understand and most of this remains in the future. How can you measure confidence in a community? Just as confidence is the root of much economic progress, so too, confidence is the glue within social cohesion; faith that if we work together, we can fix things and make for a better world. The loss of so called 'old normal' leaves many stumped for finding a definition of what 'new normal' might look like.

In my first chapter, I wrote about much going wrong with society because of our continued greed and dislocation from each other. But I now see some positives from CV19 that social commentators are starting to write and speak about. They point to the opportunity for learning a profound lesson that our ways of life were previously far too self-absorbed and focused on our species alone. This self-absorption of humanity was and remains the root cause of a potentially greater long-term threat to life than CV19 – climate change. Is it now possible that two apparently unrelated issues – viral pandemic and climate meltdown - will see a convergence of co-operative solution finding, via which we might adopt fresh and more altruistic approaches to solving both? If so, the solutions we may come up with might be arrived at very differently to the ways we would have addressed them before the current crisis. If the ultimate solutions remain the same, the means of finding them may not be. That could be exciting.

I don't have the ingredients of those solutions any more than the next person, but I have observed throughout my book that many of the factors that have been thrown into sharp relief by CV19 have been present in human communities for several decades. Fracture of society into small homogeneous groups is a product of a siloed reaction to the sheer overload of data, news and information of every kind. Far from liberating us with so much choice of information, the overload has been causing us to retreat to the familiarity of our comfort zones. Yet now, we are being abruptly ejected from that cosy state and forced by medical necessity to change lifestyle habits, leading to economic and social circumstances we do not yet understand.

We are having to adapt, invent, innovate and think outside of the normal tramlines as to how we can lead life differently. Above all, cooperation has become essential and the evidence of its effectiveness when applied properly, is all around us. That is why I see CV19 as an opportunity. Having been set widespread examples of the quiet, competent and relentless heroism of health workers doing the caring for their fellow human beings, and scientists and researchers working night and day to understand the disease better in the hope of finding ways to overcome it, those of us not in these front line roles should also be inspired to play our part. There is only one single essential for this. Cooperative behaviour and action between us and agreeing a single set of objectives between teams via enlightened leadership.

This is all fine and somewhat rhetorical for the average citizen who is not paradoxically lucky enough to be in that front line and therefore, pre-occupied with doing their duty. Duty is always easier for those who understand what that might be! What can the rest of us do to help? That question has as many answers as there are people in the world, but for me, it starts with one small step that we can all take and my book has been focusing on that subject from start to finish – seeking empathy with our fellow man and suppressing the tendency to think negatively about others as we reach out and work in harmony to solve common problems.

Let me introduce this in a fresh way – by discussing our universal tendency to hypocrisy. A recent IPSOS Mori poll in the UK found that seventy-five per cent of people believed that over the last few months, they had been observing social distancing behaviours. However, only twelve per cent thought that the majority of the population were doing the same. I grant IPSOS Mori as a reputable opinion pollster, the benefit of the doubt that they used a significant enough sample to avoid bias in the responses. So, I am less concerned here with the precise data sets, than with the massive discrepancy in perception between how people see what they are doing as opposed to their perception of what everyone else is doing.

Why is there such a gaping distance between perceptions of own behaviour and that of others? The reason has to be that we give ourselves a large amount of leeway to respond positively to questions like this but give others much less. Why? Because we know the conditions under which we make decisions and act upon them in some detail, occasionally contextualising our own mistakes to seem less bad. We know much less about other people's circumstances, with our ignorance of them increasing with distance whether geographical or cultural. This results in a lack of trust that others will be behaving as well as us and thus, a default presumption that they are not conforming to the new normal and keeping their distances.

The better we know people, the more we are likely to trust them or at least, to form our own judgements about them, either to endorse what they say, or occasionally, to know enough to dis-believe them. In a modest way, this is the beginning of empathy – to know people sufficiently to form judgements about what they claim for themselves, either true or false. All this is entirely explainable in terms of familiarity with people, but when prejudice is overlain on perception, things get complicated. There has been plenty of prejudice at large over the last few months, either to believe individual national data about CV19 infection and responses as between one government or another, or, just as commonly, to disbelieve information, purely on the basis of how we perceive that particular culture to be incompetent in such a crisis.

So, my answer to what those of us not in the medical front line can do, is to work hard to suppress our prejudices and to start trusting other people to be as well disposed to humanity and to behave as well as we believe ourselves to be behaving. If that looks like a modest agenda, given that it is about attitudes not specific actions, consider how difficult it is to change thinking on any subject! Changing attitudes may mean getting ourselves educated about how other cultures manage and order their lives. Practically speaking, that cannot always (especially now!) include traveling to new places, but at least we can read up, take notice of broadcasts and generally re-dispose ourselves to being receptive about information from far away. Don't forget, there is more information easily available than we can deal with, so we have to use our active listening and learning skills before forming judgements.

As more and more of us adopt a positive attitude towards our fellow men and women, so a benign pre-disposition to finding collective solutions to global problems will emerge more readily. If you believe that aggressive or negative behaviour repeats itself from one encounter to the next, consider that goodwill can spread just as effectively. Let's use our hyper connected world to positive effect, where everyone can watch and listen to new trends as they emerge. What am I talking about here? Why, gaining the first ingredients of empathy of course!

If I am to participate effectively in any of this noble activity, I will be calling on the sort of experience of urban master planning with which I built my career over five decades. Experience has told me time and again, that the great majority of the human race in all its cultural expressions, is positively disposed to doing good. Hopefully, my impressions from the past and confidence in the future will be matched by those with far more to offer than me and we find our way through to a better world beyond. Humans always rise to a challenge and the biggest challenges are met by the greatest and most inspired effort. There is little doubt that we need our most inspired efforts to find the new normal in our lives, but every journey, however long, requires us to make the first steps in the right direction. I hope I have helped signpost one effective pathway.